W9-BHZ-321

ADVANCED

Reader's Digest

READiNG
skill BuildER™

PROJECT EDITOR: **WARREN J. HALLIBURTON**

EDITOR: **MERLE STERN**

CONSULTANTS:

Jorge Garcia, Ed. D.
Supervisor Secondary Reading
Hillsborough County Public
Schools
Tampa, Florida

Susan Pasquini
Reading Specialist/
English Instructor
Escondido High School
San Diego, California

Frank Vernol
Instructional Learning
Secondary Reading
Dallas Independent School
District
Dallas, Texas

Grace Whittaker
Secondary Reading Supervisor
Boston Public Schools
Boston, Massachusetts

READER'S DIGEST EDUCATIONAL DIVISION
The credits and acknowledgments that appear on the inside
back cover are hereby made a part of this copyright page.
© 1980 by Reader's Digest Services, Inc., Pleasantville, N.Y. 10570. All rights reserved,
including the right to reproduce this book or parts thereof in any form.
Printed in the United States of America.

Reader's Digest ® Trademark Reg. U.S. Pat. Off. Marca Registrada ISBN 0-88300-281-6

□□□ □□□ □□□ Part 2   Reorder No. B33

silVER
EdiTiON

CONTENTS

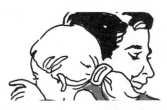
   Stories for which Audio Lessons are available.

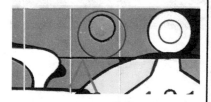

The Pleasure of Being the World's Strongest Woman

Sarah Pileggi

Kate Sandwina was a professional strong woman who performed in John Ringling's circuses in the early 1900s.

She was celebrated for performing great feats of strength, such as carrying a 600-pound (270-kilogram) cannon on her back, and lesser ones, like flipping her 160-pound (72.6-kilogram) husband Max as if he were a rifle. A handsome woman, standing 6′ 1″ (1.85 meters) and weighing 210 pounds, (95.3 kilograms) she had a narrow, corseted waist, in the style of the day, and well-rounded thighs filling out her white circus tights. Some people think she was the strongest woman who ever lived, but, because very few strong women have thought it wise to advertise their strength, the matter is difficult to judge.

In a way, Jan Todd would seem to be a direct descendant of Katie Sandwina. When she first heard of Sandwina, Jan was a naturally strong, athletically talented, intellectually well-equipped schoolgirl who took her strength for granted and worried, off and on, about her height (5′7″-1.7 meters), her weight (165 pounds-74.9 kilograms) and her posture (round shouldered).

Now Jan Todd is the strongest woman in the world—if the strength being considered is muscle strength and if it is measured in units of heavy iron. In June, 1977, in a power-lifting contest in Stephenville Crossing, Newfoundland, after four years of lifting and six months of heavy training specifically aimed at her goal, she raised a total of 1041.8 pounds (473 kilograms)—424.4 pounds (192.7 kilograms) in the squat, 176.4 pounds (80.1 kilograms) in the bench press and 441 pounds (200.2 kilograms) in the dead lift—or approximately 100 pounds (45.4 kilograms) more than any woman had ever lifted before. The total weight and two of the three lifts were world records. The third, in the bench press, was 34 pounds (15.4 kilograms) below the record held by her friend Cindy Reinhoudt of Fredonia, New York.

The bench press is a test of upper-body strength, and Todd's great power comes from her hips, legs and lower back. When she pins her long blonde hair up in a knot for a workout, buckles a wide leather belt into place over her blue sweat suit and does a deep knee bend with several hundred pounds of iron balanced on her shoulders, the power is plain to see. But at home on a farm in Nova Scotia on a Saturday morning in the fall, milking the cow, Miss Crump, harnessing an 1800-pound (817.2 kilogram) draft horse to a wagon or tossing 40-pound (18.2-kilogram) bales of hay around, is just an attractive young woman with a body admirably adapted to its labor.

The first national power-lifting championships were held in 1964 in York, Pennsylvania. An organizer of the contest and the winner in the super heavyweight division was a doctoral candidate in physical education from the University of Texas, Terry Todd, who at one time or another held 15 world records in the sport. Besides now being Jan's husband and coach, Terry is an associate professor of educational sociology at Dalhousie University in Halifax and the author of three books on strength.

Terry had been retired from competition for six years when he and Jan met at Mercer University in Macon, Georgia, a small, liberal arts school. He was a young, extremely visible associate professor of education, physical education and sociology. Jan was an active undergraduate student. "She was never afraid to try any-

Jan Todd working with heavy weights as she conditions herself for competition

thing," Terry says fondly. "I guess I admired that most about her." She worked the whole time she was in school. Active in campus politics, she edited the school newspaper for two years, and she was one of the top two or three in her class.

It was during Jan's senior year that she began lifting weights. Terry still lifted weights now and then, and Jan began to keep him company, at first working only with dumbbells to correct her round-shoulderedness, later with greater weights, but never to the point of really testing herself.

About a year after they were married, while Jan was working toward her master's degree in education, the couple went to Terry's boyhood home in Austin, Texas, for the Christmas holidays. One day as they were "taking a dose of iron pills" at the Texas Athletic Club, a very small woman entered the place and began doing dead lifts. While Jan watched, absorbed, the woman, who weighed only 113 pounds (51.3 kilograms), gradually added weight to the bar until she reached her limit—225 pounds (102.2 kilograms), twice her own weight. Jan struck up a

conversation and learned that the woman competed occasionally in the bantamweight class at men's power-lifting contests and that once she had even placed third. Before long Jan was trying some dead lifts, too, and by the time she left the gym that afternoon she had deadlifted 225 pounds (102.2 kilograms).

That evening Jan began asking Terry questions, and for the first time she heard about Katie Sandwina and the other professional strong women of circus and vaudeville. She also learned that studies have been made that indicate that women may be much closer to men in potential strength than anyone has ever believed, and that, proportionately, they may be even stronger than men in their lower bodies.

There is nothing Terry Todd does not know about weight lifting. His doctoral dissertation is entitled *A History of Progressive Resistance* and it includes a 300-page annotated bibliography. Now that Jan was curious, Terry was ready with facts, theories and lore. But what really clinched the matter for Jan was a copy of the *Guinness Book of World Records* in which she read: "The highest competitive two-handed lift by a woman is 392 lbs. (178 kilograms) by Mlle. Jane de Vesley (France) in Paris on October 14, 1926." According to Terry, Jan paused, smiled and said, "I think I can beat that. One year and four months later she did, lifting 394 ¼ pounds (179 kilograms).

"So far women have had to lift against men," said Jan recently as she bounced through the Nova Scotia countryside in her muddy car on her way to the New Germany Rural High School where she has taught 10th- and 11th-grade English for two years. "Mostly you don't win, unless you're lucky and nobody good shows up in your weight class. Until this year I had never trained with women, only with Terry. You heard about your competition through the magazines or in the mail, but you never saw them lift. Also, women were not always welcome at the men's contests."

Thanks to a man from Pennsylvania named Joe Zarella, who promoted contests of strength, there is now a national power-lifting competition for women. The first was held in April, 1977, in Nashua, New Hampshire. New Germany Rural High School was represented by a team of six girls and their 25-year-old English teacher-coach. The six were the active nucleus of a weight-lifting group Jan had launched at the school the previous fall. Sixty boys and girls had signed up, but before long the number was down to 25, mostly girls. "I was much stronger than the boys," says Jan, "and that's hard on a boy's ego at that stage of his life."

The team of six country girls who stuck it out through nearly four months of intensive weight training responded just the way their coach had hoped they would. Their concept of what was possible and appropriate for young girls to do had been expanded. When a New Hampshire television newsman asked them why they, girls, would want to lift weights, they replied that they saw no reason why they should not be strong, too.

"The schools are quite free here," said Jan. "You can take a personal approach to teaching if you want." For example, she convinced her 10th-graders that a great deal of useful knowledge of crafts and farming was stored in the heads of the old people of Lunenburg County and that, rather than let it die with them, it should be collected and made into a book. The New Germany schoolchildren fanned out through the countryside and eventually came back with a book's worth of country wisdom and knowledge.

The real focus of the Todds' lives these days, teaching and weight lifting notwithstanding, is their own piece of Lunenburg County, a 100-acre farm on top of a hill where they raise cattle and mastiffs and grow hay and vegetables. They bought it from Eldridge Milbury, who had worked the farm for 37 years and was ready to retire, but, while Milbury was building a new house nearby, he and his wife Katie stayed on to help their young understudies learn the ways of Northern farming. The four of them, working together, put up 5000 bales of hay, 1000 of them in a single day.

Jan relaxing with one of her mastiff dogs

Raising cattle often requires Jan's loving care.

Jan was always strong. Her first clue that she was unusually strong came when she was 19 years old and was in Chicago to visit her father. One day the two of them went to the Museum of Science and Industry where there was an exhibit of machines designed to test one's strength. When they tried the grip machine, Jan's grip registered slightly higher than her father's—to her amazement and his horror.

"He was 45, a roller in a steel mill and really quite strong," she says. "He was not tall, but he had big bones, big hands, broad hips. I have his build."

"If Jan had come from a wealthy family and been exposed to tennis," says Terry, "boy, she would have been good. She is naturally strong and quick." Terry was good enough at the game to go to Texas on a full tennis scholarship.

"She might also have been a good golfer or softball player or short runner," he says. "She had natural gifts, but she never had time. Lifting was the first chance she ever had to let her gifts manifest themselves."

Jan was in her kitchen one evening, shucking corn from the garden, making faces because it was full of fat worms and trying to explain herself. "I lift because I love it," she said. "I love the way it makes me feel. It has extended my idea of the limits of what is possible for me. If someone had told me four years ago that I would squat with 400 pounds (181.6 kilograms) on my shoulders, I would not have believed it. Lifting was a whole new world. It is hard to explain, but it became something I wanted to try for."

Jan Todd has never worn spangles and tights. She has never heard the cheers of thousands as Katie Sandwina once had. And she has never made a dime from having been, for a while, the strongest woman in the world. But it really doesn't matter. There will always be some people who understand what she did, and a few, like Terry, will even understand why.

Number of Words: 1843 ÷ _____ Minutes Reading Time = Rate _____

Tending horses is one of Jan's most satisfying farm chores.

I. SUMMARY

Check √ the sentence below that best summarizes the story.

_____ 1. Born in Florida, Jan Todd went on to become an excellent farmer in Nova Scotia.

_____ 2. Encouraged by her weightlifting husband, Jan Todd has developed into the world's strongest woman.

_____ 3. A natural athlete, Jan Todd could have excelled in many sports such as golf, softball and the short run.

_____ 4. As the world's strongest woman, Jan Todd puts her strength to practical use on the farm.

10 points for correct answer   SCORE: _____

II. FACT/OPINION

Some of the sentences below state facts. Others express opinions that may or may not be true. Write F before each sentence that states a fact and O before each that gives an opinion.

_____ 1. Without Terry's help Jan would never have set the world's record.

_____ 2. Jan's strength comes from her hips, her legs and her lower back.

_____ 3. Women have not always been welcome as competitors in men's weightlifting contests.

_____ 4. There is no reason why women should not want to lift weights and be strong, too.

_____ 5. If Jan had come from a wealthy family, she would have been good at tennis or golf.

10 points for each correct answer   SCORE: _____

III. MAIN IDEA

Check ✓ *the one statement that best describes what the story is about.*

_____ **1.** Jan Todd lifts weights because she loves to.

_____ **2.** Being a weightlifter has helped Jan Todd become one of the best farmers in Nova Scotia.

_____ **3.** More and more women are becoming weightlifters.

20 points for correct answer   SCORE: _____

IV. AUTHOR'S PURPOSE

Check ✓ *the four statements below that help explain why the author wrote the story.*

_____ **1.** to show us that women, as well as men, can enjoy the sport of weightlifting

_____ **2.** to describe some events in Jan Todd's life and how she came to power-lift a record 1042 pounds

_____ **3.** to show us how being a weightlifter has made Jan a very unconventional person

_____ **4.** to give us an idea of the pleasures Jan derives from being strong and athletic

_____ **5.** to show us that Jan, though she chose an unusual sport to compete in, is a fulfilled, normal person

5 points for each correct answer   SCORE: _____

PERFECT TOTAL SCORE: 100   TOTAL SCORE: _____

V. QUESTION FOR THOUGHT

How do you feel about the fact that women are now taking up sports that until recently were for men only? Support your viewpoint with reasons, examples and facts.

Maine's Frozen Couple

Edward Rowe Snow

In the year 1850, one of the strangest events in the history of Maine occurred near Owl's Head, one of the state's most beautiful lighthouses. In a strong gale on December 22, no fewer than five staunch vessels were wrecked along the rocky coast between Owl's Head Light and Spruce Head, where that night the temperature went far below zero, and the wrecks and the shoreline were heavily encased in ice before morning.

Before the storm began, a coasting schooner had been anchored in the vicinity of Jameson's Point across the bay. The schooner was without its captain, who had either abandoned the vessel because of a premonition or had decided not to make the trip for personal reasons. Some persons claimed that he had been relieved of his command by the owner of the schooner. For whatever reason, the captain was absent when the storm broke, and the only people on board the schooner were the two members of the crew—Richard B. Ingraham and Roger Elliott—and Ingraham's fiancée, Lydia Dyer, whom the owner had allowed to go aboard for the journey to Boston. As soon as the storm

struck, Lydia Dyer went below and retired for the evening.

The gale increased hour by hour. By 11 o'clock the schooner was in great difficulty. Suddenly, a few moments before midnight, the cables snapped and the schooner began her journey across the bay toward Owl's Head. Clearing Owl's Head itself, she piled up on the cruel ledges to the southward, and the rocks soon pierced her hull in several places. The craft filled and settled in a rocky cradle just a short distance offshore.

When the schooner hit, Lydia Dyer rushed up on deck, carrying a comforter and a large blanket. Richard quickly wrapped them around her as protection from the driving snow and icy surf. Ingraham and Elliott tried to decide what to do before high tide, which would arrive in something more than an hour. Ingraham located a sheltered part of the deck against the rail around the ship's stern, and there they crouched to get some protection from the wind and waves. But with the tide coming in, the spray and surf dashed with increasing fury against the helpless trio, drenching them thoroughly. Their clothing began to stiffen, freezing to their bodies. Richard Ingraham, standing by the stern's rail, realized that there was little chance of their living through the night unless he could arrange some better shelter at once. The wind was still rising, and the tide was almost high.

"Lydia," Dick said to his sweetheart, "I don't have to tell you that we're in great danger, but I've thought of a plan that may save our lives."

"I'll do whatever you say," Lydia answered.

Dick continued. "Put the blanket down as close as you can get to the rail and then lie down on it and pull it around yourself."

Lydia did as directed, and when she had pulled the blanket around her back, Dick placed himself beside her, pulled his own blanket around both of them and wrapped his arms firmly around her wet, icy body. Then Elliott crawled in beside Dick, forced himself as close as he could and pulled the old comforter around him. Although he believed that Ingraham was right in suggesting that they all huddle together for the night to keep alive, Elliott took the precaution of making sure that his sheath knife was handy to chip the ice away so they could breathe.

By this time it was dead high tide, and the wind was stronger than before. Every wave was breaking over the entire hull of the schooner. The blankets and comforter were hidden under a frozen mass of salt ice, which, because of the sub-zero temperature, soon hardened into a solid ice cake. By three o'clock that morning the waves were still breaking over the vessel, and the icy covering was inches thick. Finally the young couple lost consciousness. The ice jacket kept the air away from them.

Elliott, however, who was a cautious and determined man, kept picking away at a small opening in the ice cake near his face. In this way he was able to breathe. Then, although the three prisoners under the ice-cap did not know it, the tide began to turn and go out, and, as often happens, the storm went down with the tide. The sun rose a few hours later, and Elliott, seeing the glow, began to hack and chop in earnest.

Soon he had punched his knife through enough of the ice to break off a section 6 inches (15.24 centimeters) thick, and by squeezing and clubbing with his hands and pushing against the edges he squirmed his way through the narrow opening in the ice covering and landed on the slippery deck. His hands were cut and bleeding, and he rested for a moment before his next move.

Elliott looked at his companions frozen under the shelter of the railing. The ice was at least 6 inches (15.24 centimeters) thick over their bodies. There was no movement at all. It appeared that they had frozen to death! This panicked him into action. He stumbled over to the side of the ship and looked down upon the rocks below. It was dead low tide, and to his amazement he realized that he could walk ashore.

By this time the schooner had broken in two, and Elliott climbed down through the break to reach the rocks and begin his journey toward civilization. But the rocks were icy and extremely slippery. His stiffened clothing was an enormous hindrance, too. He stumbled and staggered over the rocks, falling at almost every step. Finally, the temptation to remain where he fell and to rest before he went on proved too much.

Elliott relaxed against a giant boulder and fell into a deep sleep. It was a sleep from which he might never have awakened, but luck was with him. The tide was turning. Soon it began to come in, and a giant wave splashed over the sleeping man. The icy wave revived him—and saved his life.

Elliott tried to scramble to his feet, but the effort was too sudden. He toppled over backward, hitting his head as he fell. The shock, however, helped to bring him to his senses, and he got up again, this time more slowly and deliberately. Eventually, after agonizing minutes of tortured walking, he reached the high-tide mark, where giant snowdrifts blocked his way.

Foot by foot, yard by yard, Elliott broke a path through the drifts until he finally reached a road. He had no way of knowing where the nearest house was located or in what direction he should turn. The tracks of a box sled with the hoofmarks of a horse decided his course. He would follow the tracks until he reached help. Turning to the right, he started along the road that actually led to Owl's Head Light.

Now upright, now falling, Elliott made slow but steady progress. He did not know how much longer he could continue in his weakened condititon. Then, through the cold morn-

ing air he heard the sound of bells. He looked up and thought he saw a sleigh coming toward him along the road. A minute later he realized that a box sled was drawing closer to him. With a half-cry Elliott collapsed in the road.

The driver of the sled was William Masters, keeper of Owl's Head Light. Masters lifted Elliott onto the sled and drove toward the lighthouse. He took the freezing man inside and cut the stiffened clothing from his body. He forced a hot drink down his throat and put him to bed, covered with blankets, comforters and quilts. But even in his semiconscious condition, Elliott remembered that there was a message he should give to the lighthouse keeper immediately. With a tremendous effort he opened his eyes and tried to get up.

"Take it easy there," Masters continued. "You've had a hard time of it. Just lie back and go to sleep." Elliott was not to be denied, however, and opened his mouth to speak.

"Others are on the wreck," he gasped faintly. "Please get them."

"All right," Masters assured him. "We'll leave at once. Now you go to sleep."

A moment later Elliott was so deeply asleep that he didn't hear the lighthouse bell signaling every ablebodied man in the countryside to leave his home and aid in rescue work. Soon Masters' sled with a dozen men aboard was following Elliott's tracks back to the shore. The wreck out on the rocks was quickly sighted.

By now the tide was well on the way in. It was quite a task to reach the broken vessel, but the men waded out and clambered aboard. They began to hack away at the two bodies frozen in the ice beside the railing and soon had them severed from the deck. But the tide was rising, and they had to work fast. Ten strong men moved the heavy ice cake containing the young couple over to the break in the deck and handed it down to others waiting below in waist-deep surf. The men of Owl's Head then carried their icy burden ashore in the bitter cold and loaded it onto the sled.

"They're both dead, all right," exclaimed one of the men.

"I'm afraid so," answered Masters, "but we've got to try to bring them back to life."

The huge ice cake was brought into the kitchen of the nearest house, and, by careful thawing and chipping, the ice was completely removed from the blankets that covered the bodies. Cold-water applications were then administered, with the water as near freezing as possible. The temperature of the water was slowly raised, until eventually it was approximately 55 degrees Fahrenheit (10 degrees Centigrade). The next step was to move the hands and feet of the victims, slowly at first, and then at a more rapid rate. Their bodies were massaged, first gently and then vigorously for half an hour.

Lydia was the first to show signs of life, stirring slightly after two hours of constant attention. Ingraham took almost a full hour longer to respond to the treatment, but he finally moved uneasily and opened his eyes.

"What is all this? Where are we?" he asked and they told him the whole story. He looked across at Lydia, and she smiled at him faintly.

After Lydia and Ingraham were covered with extra blankets and fed hot drinks, they fell asleep. On the following day they were well enough to eat, but it was many, many weeks before they could get up and walk about. It was spring before they had completely recovered.

The state of Richard's finances prevented his marrying Lydia at once, but eventually they married and had four children. One of their descendants is living today at Whitestone, New York—Mrs. Louise Thompson Squires.

Roger Elliott never fully recovered from the effects of his terrible experience. Although he did not go to sea again, he frequently visited the Rockland waterfront, where he told and retold his fascinating story.

The episode of the frozen couple was declared a miracle and discussed for years afterward around the fireplaces up and down the Maine coast. Whether the couple actually froze to death and were thawed back to life is a question that is still debated.

Number of Words: 1912 ÷ _____ Minutes Reading Time = Rate _____

I. SUPPORTING DETAILS

Circle the letter (a, b or c) before the answer that best completes each of the sentences below.

1. The story takes place near the _____ lighthouse.
   a. West Quoddy   b. Owl's Head   c. Jameson Point

2. In the storm, the spray and surf turned into a _____.
   a. giant wave   b. freezing rain   c. solid ice cake

3. Roger Elliott stumbled ashore and was found by _____.
   a. the ship's captain
   b. the lighthouse keeper
   c. a farmer

4. The two frozen bodies were revived by _____.
   a. slowly thawing them out
   b. placing them near a fire
   c. forcing hot rum down their throats

5 points for each correct answer   SCORE: _____

II. CAUSE/EFFECT

Match each cause in column A to its effect in column B. Write the letter in the space provided.

A	B
_____ 1. Because the gale snapped the cables	a. the ship was soon under a heavy ice covering.
_____ 2. Because the temperature was so low	b. the ice jacket could be chipped at and broken.
_____ 3. Because Elliott kept his sheath knife handy	c. the ship ran aground near the shore.
_____ 4. Because a giant wave splashed over Elliott	d. the exhausted man was revived.

10 points for each correct answer   SCORE: _____

III. STORY ELEMENTS

The author conveys both how dangerous the event in the story was and how incredible its outcome. Check ✓ the four sentences below that explain how he does this.

_____ **1.** He describes in detail the fury of the storm and its effect on the schooner.

_____ **2.** He gives us an idea of how desperate the situation was for the three passengers on board.

_____ **3.** He compares the terrifying experience of the three people to other events in their lives.

_____ **4.** He shows how hard it was for even one of the people to get away from the ship.

_____ **5.** He tells us how miraculous people thought it was that the couple was brought back to life.

_____ **6.** He describes how it is impossible for a person, once frozen, to be brought back to life.

10 points for each correct answer   SCORE: _____

PERFECT TOTAL SCORE: 100   TOTAL SCORE: _____

IV. QUESTIONS FOR THOUGHT

What unusual story have you ever been told or heard? Why do you believe it happened or never happened?

Gone to the Dogs

Ron Rosenbaum

Writer seeks THE original shaggy-dog story (must be about shaggy dog). Also seeks good shaggy-dog stories about anything at all. Fifty- dollar reward for best in each category.

There's this down-and-out guy in a cafe in Kansas City. He finds a copy of the London *Times* on the chair next to him. Don't ask me what it's doing there. He notices one particular classified ad—this is back when the classifieds were on the front page of *The Times*.

"Generous Reward Offered," says the ad, "for return of runaway dog. Large, brown and white. Exceedingly shaggy." Well, the guy doesn't think anything more about it until he goes out the cafe door. What does he see wagging its tail on the sidewalk across the street?

That's how the original shaggy-dog story begins. I'm sure of it. For years I've been hearing all sorts of long-winded jokes described as shaggy-dog stories. Some were funny, some not

so funny. But not one had the least bit to do with a shaggy dog. It began to occur to me that there must be an *exceedingly* funny shaggy-dog story that actually featured a shaggy dog, a story so hilarious it gave the name "shaggy-dog story" to a series of stories that developed into a joke style and then was lost beneath the thicket of shaggy stories it inspired. I wanted to find that lost joke.

So I did what the Englishman who had lost his shaggy dog did: I wrote a classified ad offering a reward for the lost shaggy-dog story. I ran the ad in 10 publications.

As the letters began coming in, I ran into some discouraging warnings from the self-proclaimed experts in the shaggy-dog field.

The undisputed giant of

shaggy-dog research is Professor Jan Harold Brunvand of the University of Utah. Back in 1963, the *Journal of American Folklore* published the professor's massive systematization of all known shaggy-dog stories, classified according to something called the "Stith Thompson *Motif-Index of Folk Literature*." In his deadly serious article entitled "A Classification for Shaggy Dog Stories," which reads like an elaborate academic shaggy-dog joke all by itself, the professor warns that "it is fruitless to inquire whether any given joke was the forerunner of the current shaggy-dog stories." The professor speaks condescendingly of "the widely held idea that the first such joke must have been about a dog that was shaggy."

Well it wasn't about a *parrot* that was shaggy. And it wasn't

about a dog that was smooth. It seemed to me that there must be something about the shagginess and the dogginess of the first shaggy-dog story that made it a particularly fitting, in fact the inevitable, name for the writing style.

Meanwhile, back in Kansas City, this down-and-out guy sees that across the street from him is a large, shaggy, brown-and-white dog. Exceedingly shaggy. As a matter of fact, the shaggiest dog he's ever come upon. Back into the cafe he runs to grab that copy of *The Times* with its precious ad. He notes the address:

Lord Peter Brearly
Brearly Hall
Belgravia
London SW1

Back out of the cafe he runs, grabs the huge shaggy dog by the collar and together they set off for London.

But before we get any further, let me concede that this shaggy-dog story I'm telling isn't the only shaggy-dog story about a shaggy dog. Several people have sent me a series of long, drawn-out jokes about "shaggy-dog contests," and, while I do not think they predate the lost-dog, shaggy-dog tale I'm interrupting, one of

them at least bears repeating in a shortened form:

A man with an incredibly shaggy dog enters his beast in a local contest to determine the shaggiest dog in town. When the three local judges see the dog, one after another they exclaim, "Shaggiest dog I've ever seen." Dog wins first prize, enters state shaggy-dog contest. Same overwhelmed response from each of the three state judges. Winning first prize again, dog enters nationwide contest, then worldwide contest. Same astonished reactions from judges, same prizewinning results. Dog proceeds to enter and win solar-system-wide contest, then galaxy-wide contest, amazing entire planets and constellations with his shagginess. Dog finally enters contest for shaggiest dog in the universe. First alien judge: "That's the shaggiest dog I've ever seen." Second alien judge: "Shaggiest dog I've ever seen." Third alien judge: "He's not that shaggy."

I received letters with stories about shaggy dogs that talk in cafes, shaggy dogs that walk on water, shaggy dogs that walk underwater, shaggy dogs that play the piano, play baseball and multiply three-digit numbers in no time flat.

But none of these, I declare, is the *original* shaggy-dog story. In each of these stories another animal would do just as well as a shaggy dog. A hairy-ape contest is not inconceivable. There is no shortage of kangaroos talking in cafes. And piano-playing horses are plentiful. None of these jokes *needs* a shaggy dog. The fact that a shaggy dog makes a guest appearance in the lead role merely attests to the comic notoriety already established for all shaggy dogs by the original shaggy-dog story.

It's a long journey from the cafe in Kansas City to Brearly Hall in London. The man has no money (neither does the dog), so they hop a freight to Chicago, hitch a ride on a flatbed truck to New York City and stow away on a freighter bound for Liverpool. They climb ashore half starved—the man has given the dog every scrap of food he can beg to keep him healthy and shaggy. They sleep out in the cold before they can get a lift to London. They get lost in the city, get bad directions, get further lost, get correct directions but follow them faultily.

I could go on like this forever, as some shaggy-dog-storytellers do—piling digression on digression, producing so many irrelevant details that the simple kernel of the joke becomes obscured beneath all that shag. Of course only experienced storytellers should attempt exceedingly shaggy shaggy-dog stories. If not told flawlessly, they can become such embarrassing experiences to the teller that the humiliation will haunt the would-be wit for so long it becomes a case of the tale that dogs the wag.

At last the man and his incredibly shaggy companion find their way to the tall iron gate of Brearly Hall. The man rings the bell on the gate. Time passes. At last a servant emerges. He looks at the bedraggled man and the incredibly shaggy dog and raises his eyebrows.

"Take me to Lord Peter Brearly right away," croaks the

exhausted man from Kansas City.

The servant allows the dog and the man inside the gate but tells them to wait there. He disappears inside the house. Time passes. Finally he returns, accompanied by the butler. The butler looks at the man and the dog and raises his eyebrows slightly.

"Take me to Lord Peter Brearly right away," the man pleads urgently, thinking of the "generous reward," hot bath, clean clothes and good food he can look forward to.

The butler tells the man that Lord Brearly is in the middle of a croquet game with friends and has issued standing orders that he is not to be disturbed until the final wicket. The butler tells the man to be seated on the steps and wait. The butler disappears. Time passes.

And speaking of time, the most difficult question to answer about this original shaggy-dog story I'm telling you is exactly how old it is. Most people who sent me a version of this story traced it back to the mid-1930s. A Miss Georgiana Remer sent in a joke about a shaggy dog she claimed she heard in 1930 or 1931, while she was attending Horace Mann High School in the Bronx.

First man, addressing stranger in street: "That's a shaggy dog you've got there."

Second man: "Oh, I don't know. . . . It's right shaggy though."

While this is not an all-time blockbuster of a shaggy-dog story, it does suggest that the original shaggy-dog story must have been around in the late 1920s in order to have given birth to such abbreviated offspring.

Croquet match completed, Lord Brearly himself finally appears at the door of his town house, accompanied by the butler carrying his croquet mallet.

"Lord Peter Brearly," the man cries out. "You're Lord Peter Brearly."

"I am," says Lord Brearly.

"The one who put the ad in *The Times* about losing a large brown-and-white dog, exceedingly shaggy."

"Yes," says Lord Brearly.

"Well I have your dog," says the man pushing the shaggy creature up to Lord Brearly.

"I daresay my dog was exceedingly shaggy," Lord Brearly says, "but not *that* shaggy."

That's it, the original shaggy-dog story. Not that shaggy. Not that funny, I'm afraid.

When the weight of the available evidence convinced me that this story and no other story was in fact the original shaggy-dog story, I was exceedingly disappointed. Shaggy-dog stories are about disappointment. Disappointed by the punch line, one becomes amused at how disappointed one is, then finally disappointed that one is not *that* amused. Like the man who brought the dog to London, the listener who puts up with all the shag along the way expects a "generous reward" at the tail end of the journey and ends up getting so little that it's laughable.

Shaggy-dog stories about disappointments that come after expectations are exceeded beyond anyone's wildest dreams. There is "The Horse That Tried Out for Leo Durocher." Horse talks baseball manager Durocher into giving him a tryout so he can prove he's a superb ballplayer. Horse gets up at bat, slams home runs. Horse gets out in field, makes diving catches, shows fancy footwork on double-play piv-ots. Then Leo asks horse to try pitching. Horse trots off field. Leo runs after, asks horse what's the matter. "What's the *matter*?" says the horse. "Who ever heard of a horse pitching for a baseball team?"

But—much to the disappointment of some of you, I'm sure—the story of the original shaggy-dog isn't quite complete yet. One element remains a mystery. Place of birth. A matter of no small consequence as we shall see. Americans assume the story was conceived in America. (The story I've been telling is obviously an American version.)

But Professor Eric Partridge puts forth a version of "the original shaggy-dog story" that is unmistakably British. His version seethes with disapproval of American excess, its shagginess if you will.

However, the story probably originates in America. For only in America can this wild shaggy celebration of excess still be found. Only in America can such rough beasts slouch along the streets at large.

Number of Words: 1827 ÷ _____ Minutes Reading Time = Rate _____

I. STORY ELEMENTS

The author conveys very well the sense of what a shaggy-dog story is. Check ✓ the four sentences below that explain how he does this.

_____ **1.** He tells a long and typical shaggy-dog story himself.

_____ **2.** He often interrupts the story with side discussions and irrelevant details.

_____ **3.** He compares shaggy-dog stories with other types of jokes.

_____ **4.** He makes us impatient to know how the story ends.

_____ **5.** He delivers the punch line in a mild, weak manner.

_____ **6.** He explains at great length why so many people like shaggy-dog stories.

5 points for each correct answer   SCORE: _____

II. INFERENCES

Check ✓ the three sentences below that can be inferred from the story.

_____ **1.** The author admires previous serious studies on shaggy-dog humor.

_____ **2.** Shaggy-dog stories are by far the most popular jokes.

_____ **3.** A shaggy-dog story is not supposed to be too funny.

_____ **4.** A shaggy-dog story should be as drawn out as possible.

_____ **5.** It takes a special sense of humor to enjoy such stories.

5 points for each correct answer   SCORE: _____

III. VOCABULARY

Circle the letter (a, b or c) before the definition that matches the meaning of the underlined word in each sentence.

1. The professor wrote a *monograph* about humor.
   a. scholarly article   **b.** cartoon   **c.** phonograph

2. A hairy-ape contest would not be *inconceivable*.
   a. successful   **b.** popular   **c.** unthinkable

3. The servant looked at the *bedraggled* man in amazement.
   a. strange   **b.** wet and dirty   **c.** tired

10 points for each correct answer   SCORE: _____

IV. SUMMARY

Check √ the seven items listed below that can be included in a summary of the main shaggy-dog story told by the author.

_____ **1.** dog sitting in a bar	_____ **6.**	dog and man
_____ **2.** a man reading a newspaper		travel far
_____ **3.** an ad for the return of	_____ **7.**	by car and plane
a shaggy dog	_____ **8.**	arrive in London
_____ **4.** a talking dog	_____ **9.**	return the dog to
_____ **5.** man sees a shaggy dog		Lord Brearly
	_____ **10.**	it is the wrong dog

5 points for each correct answer   SCORE: _____

PERFECT TOTAL SCORE: 100   TOTAL SCORE: _____

V. QUESTION FOR THOUGHT

Which type of humor (pun, slapstick, cartoon, etc.) do you find most funny? Explain your reasons.

The television special was going according to script—as is expected in commercial television. But the two guests from *Sesame Street*, Maria and Big Bird, clearly were not accustomed to being restrained by a script, and at a particularly happy moment in the performance the two joined hands and broke into a spontaneous dance.

"No, no, no!" the director shrieked, his arms flailing like the wings of a mortally wounded bird. Then, controlling his outburst, he murmured, "Stop, stop. You are not following the script. Nowhere does it say to ad-lib. Nowhere does it say 'Maria, grab Big Bird and dance.'" He muttered something about what their antics were doing to the camera angle.

"But it's the way we feel!" Sonia Manzano (Maria) explained, her laughter reflecting the happiness that had inspired the improvisation.

The director looked at her with starched amazement.

"We always express the way we feel on Sesame Street," Sonia went on to explain.

Big Bird was nodding in agreement.

The director nodded, too, but not in agreement; he seemed to

Sonia's Street of Dreams

Warren Halliburton

be considering the reaction to the unrehearsed peformance. Apparently the stage hands, technicians, and everyone around had enjoyed it. The director may not have been convinced that the scene was better played for Sonia and Big Bird's reacting to the spirit of the script, but he knew it had seemed more appealing.

"You can always edit out what you don't want," Sonia suggested.

"All right," the director agreed. "We'll play the scene again—the same way." And the *Sesame Street* players began again to do their professional thing—to improvise as they do for their regular educational program, but this time for a special network production.

What had won out over the restraints of script and time was the feeling of family, of one performer relating and responding to the other. This contagion of feeling characterizes *Sesame Street*—a nationally renowned television program for preschool youngsters that entertains while teaching them the basic skills of reading and arithmetic. Showcasing a talented group of children who act, sing and dance, *Sesame Street* also features a "family" of delightful characters, such as Big Bird, Cookie Monster, Kermit-the-Frog, Bert, Ernie, Oscar-the-Grouch and Grover—all distinctly individual and colorful muppets.

Among the "living" young people on *Sesame Street* are David, Susan, Gordon, Mr. Hooper, Bob, Linda, Luis, Olivia and Maria, the last one played by Sonia Manzano.

Playing on *Sesame Street* could be a unique experience for any performer: an opportunity to relate to children, to other adult actors and, of course, to the muppets. Such interaction takes a special talent, one that is right down Sonia Manzano's street—the one located in the South Bronx, where she grew up.

"Just about everyone in the neighborhood was treated as family," she remembers. That's the way the community was, not too many years ago, for this young actress. She describes the relationship of these residents with obvious affection. "If I got into any mischief, like playing on the rocks down the block, my mother was sure to find out. Each mother was everybody's mother. There was always some parent around to keep an eye on us. That's why we were able to go out at night and play until ten o'clock. All my mother had to do was check to see a parent outside, and she knew I was going to be looked after."

But Sonia's childhood was not all fun and games. As a youngster living in a predominantly Puerto Rican community, she was impressed with how different her life was from the lives of the people she learned about in the books at school. "They lived in the country and had pretty white picket fences and green lawns. We lived in old tenements with dirty sidewalks out front. And the fathers in the books all went to work in suits, white shirts and bright ties, while the mothers stayed at home. My father didn't wear a white shirt or any tie at all when he went to work, and my mother didn't stay at home; she went to work, too."

Sonia recalls these differences with amusement now. But they were important differences and not so amusing to a young girl growing up, and they created frustrating experiences in school. What was worse, some things Sonia learned caused her to question the wisdom of her loving parents. The teacher said a good breakfast consisted of such things as milk, whole-wheat bread and eggs. But all the breakfast she and her sister and two brothers were given was coffee and Italian bread.

Distracted by these differences, Sonia did poorly in her schoolwork and received barely passing grades. She was saved, however, by her interest in reading, which she pursued with such enthusiasm that she was occasionally asked to stop while the rest of the class caught up. "That was really something," she exclaims, as if reliving these elementary school days. But she is quick to point out that none of her childhood was lived with any sense of tragedy. "Kids don't feel any of that," she observes, and, she might add, neither do positive-thinking adults such as Sonia Manzano. That is why she can recognize the bitter and accept it with the sweet.

Even when Sonia was a young girl growing up in the Bronx, she had a rich, creative mind that imagined what it could not explain. She imagined that coffee and Italian bread must have been better for her than milk and eggs, otherwise her mother would not have given them to her morning after morning. Even the pictures that showed Santa Claus coming down the chimney could have proved troublesome, since the Manzano family had no chimney in their tenement (nor did any one else Sonia knew), but Sonia imagined Santa magically entering her house through a window.

A girl with such a spirited imagination and spunky personality could not go through school unnoticed, and Sonia didn't. One of her junior high-school teachers encouraged her to take the test for the High

School of Performing Arts in Manhattan—a special school reserved for a few talented students who are admitted on a competitive basis. Sonia accepted the challenge, ignoring the discouraging remarks of her friends and the critical silence of her family. She gave a dramatic reading and was accepted.

It was easier for Sonia to get into the high school, though, than it was to stay there. Academically, she went from top to bottom. That is, she had always been potentially, if not actually, at the top of her class before, but now she had to work to catch up and keep up. Meanwhile she was learning of another more privileged way of life, meeting girls who went to Europe for vacation and enrolled in private dance classes for recreation instead of having to hang around the block or work—if they were lucky.

Struggling to keep up with her new classmates, Sonia

Sonia with two favorite Sesame Street characters, muppets Oscar (above) and Bert (right)

formed her first real, specific ambition—to attend college. Why not me, she secretly thought; everybody else is going! But she was not surprised that her counselor did not recommend her, certainly not to any one of the three most prestigious colleges in the performing arts. It figured; she had been given to understand that Carnegie-Mellon, Northwestern and Juilliard were for the academically privileged only. Her counselor's recommendation was an honor that Sonia simply had not earned, not with her modest grades. All right, she thought, I'll recommend myself. So Sonia applied on her own and was accepted to Carnegie-Mellon—on a partial scholarship, too.

By her third year, Sonia was performing in the school production of *Godspell*. She was then offered the opportunity of going to New York, which she accepted, on the condition that she receive course credit.

While playing in *Godspell*, the student actress was approached by an agent who suggested that she try out for *Sesame Street*. Although she had no particular training or experience to qualify her for the show, she was one of the few selected for a regular part.

Pleased as she is now to be a member of the cast of *Sesame Street*, Sonia sees it as only the beginning of her career. She is young and talented, and she aspires to greater show-business success. She is also intelligent, sensitive and Puerto Rican, which gives her a particular understanding as well as certain frustrations. One frustration is the one-dimensional roles for Puerto Ricans, which stereotype them as either island innocents or barrio toughs, who speak with Spanish accents even if they are native born. But, Sonia realizes, it is the same with most television characters, who are stereotypes too; so why should she take exception? The condition is unfortunate, she knows, "But," as she says, "it's where we are."

Meanwhile, Sonia is working hard to change things. During the six months of the year that she is not busy with *Sesame Street*, she tries her hand at directing and works with young Puerto Rican theater groups. She sees these groups as very much a part of her future, as the source for scripts and productions for "people like me," as she calls them.

Then there is Sonia the very private person, the one who, as a schoolgirl, was introduced to a life quite different from her own and was sometimes confused by the conflicts. But both were equally real, and the differences forced her to cope in a way that prepared her well. Sonia is still having to cope with different ways of living—with the glamour of show life, successful people and swank parties on one hand and, on the other hand, the reality of Latin ties with family and friends in the old neighborhood. Both are important for Sonia to maintain, and she has found a place for both.

The upper West Side of Manhattan, where she lives, is a far cry from the old neighborhood. Here nobody knows his or her neighbor, unlike the neighborhood of her childhood with its extended family. But here this thoughtful young actress has privacy to reflect on who she is and where she is going.

Number of Words: 1704 ÷ _____ Minutes Reading Time = Rate _____

I. MAIN IDEA

Check √ the one statement that best describes the selection.

_____ **1.** *Sesame Street* is such a popular show.

_____ **2.** Being in show business has spoiled Sonia Manzano.

_____ **3.** Sonia remains unspoiled despite her success.

10 points for correct answer   SCORE: _____

II. OUTLINING

Complete the outline of the selection by writing the letter (a, b, c, d or e) for each of the following sentences in its proper place.

 a. The director objected when Sonia did not stick to the script.
 b. Sonia now leads a busy, satisfying life.
 c. At school, Sonia realized that her upbringing was different.
 d. They improvised a dance, as they do on *Sesame Street.*
 e. On her own, Sonia won a scholarship to college.

 I. Sonia and Big Bird were guests on a television special.
  A. _____
  B. _____
 II. Sonia's life serves as an inspiration.
  A. _____
  B. She went to the High School of Performing Arts.
  C. _____
  D. She won a part on *Sesame Street.*
 III. _____
  A. She works on *Sesame Street* for six months of the year.
  B. She works with Puerto Rican theater groups.

10 points for each correct answer   SCORE: _____

III. PROBLEM SOLVING

Circle the letter (a, b or c) for the answer that describes the solution to each of the following problems.

1. Sonia improvised a dance that was not in the script.
   a. The director told her to follow the script exactly.
   b. The director gave up and let her dance on the show.
   c. The director adjusted the camera angles.

2. As a child, Sonia wanted to play in the street.
   a. There was always someone's parent to keep an eye on her.
   b. Her mother would not let her stay outside after dark.
   c. Her mother could see her by looking out the window.

3. What Sonia got for breakfast was different from what children were supposed to eat, according to the school books.
   a. As a young girl, she was amused by the differences.
   b. She liked to imagine that what she got was better for her.
   c. She ate milk and eggs while in school.

4. Sonia did not do well in school.
   a. She recognized and accepted her limitations.
   b. She tried to remain unnoticed by her teachers.
   c. She became an enthusiastic reader.

10 points for each correct answer   SCORE: _____

PERFECT TOTAL SCORE: 100   TOTAL SCORE: _____

IV. QUESTION FOR THOUGHT

Have you ever thought about a career in TV? Explain the reasons why you would or would not want such a career.

Deep Sea Search

Robert F. Marx

In April 1502 Columbus set sail from Spain with four small ships on his fourth and last voyage of discovery. It was to be his most dangerous and least profitable voyage and one that caused him such anguish that he died soon after the voyage came to its disastrous end. His intentions were not only to seek gold and other precious objects but also to search for a strait along the area of Central America that he believed would permit him to reach the riches of the Orient. After arriving in the Caribbean, he spent almost a year cruising along the Central American coasts, discovering very little of importance. Sea worms caused such damage to the hulls of his small ships that two of them were stripped and scuttled.

Since his two remaining ships—*Capitana* and *Santiago*—were also in very bad condition, he finally admitted failure and started home. He headed for Santo Domingo where he hoped to repair both ships before attempting to sail for Spain. By the time he was between Cuba and Jamaica, he and his crewmen were suffering from a shortage of water and food, and both ships were leaking badly. Columbus' son, Ferdinand, who chronicled the voyage, wrote: "Day and night we never ceased working three pumps in each ship, and if any broke down, we had to supply its place by bailing with kettles while it was being patched up."

With their ships so full of water, they made slow progress, but when the wind swung around to the east, blowing from the direction toward which they were trying to sail, that was the final straw. On June 25, 1503, the discouraged Columbus entered St. Anne's Bay, which he called "Santa Gloria," on the north coast of Jamaica, and ran both of his ships aground, "about a bow-shot distance from shore." The bay was not new to Columbus for he had stopped there in 1494 on his second voyage. The ships were run up close to two freshwater streams and an Indian village from which he hoped to obtain a supply of food. There were 116 hungry mouths to feed on the two ships. With only the forecastle or front end and stern or rear end castles sticking above the surface of the water, there were insufficient accommodations for such a large number of men, and tents were erected on the main decks, which were probably awash at high tide.

Soon after his arrival Columbus purchased a dugout canoe from the Indians and sent crewmen in it to Santo Domingo to notify the authorities of his plight. However, the governor of Santa Domingo was his enemy and delayed aid, so it was a year and five days before Columbus and his men were rescued. Things went well during the beginning of his enforced stay, for the Indians were very happy to trade food for glass beads and other items of barter. However, after the Indians had an accumulation of these items, they supplied less and less food to the Spaniards. When months passed and no aid arrived, several members of the expedition enlisted the majority of the men in a mutiny and plotted to assassinate Columbus, blaming him for all their miseries. Columbus, though bedridden with painful arthritis, was able to put down the mutiny in its early stages.

When Columbus and his men finally sailed from St. Anne's Bay for Santo Domingo on June 29, 1504, leaving behind the two worthless ships, he was a discouraged and heartbroken man, and he died not long after his arrival in Spain. Before dying, he had extracted a promise from Ferdinand to found a city near the spot of his enforced stay in St. Anne's Bay. In 1509 Ferdinand had a group of colonists sent there from Santo Domingo, and the town of New Seville was founded several hundred yards from where the two wrecks lay. But the surrounding swamps made the area very unhealthy, and the town was moved to the south coast of Jamaica 20 years later, in 1529.

From the book written by Ferdinand and from other contemporary documents, the location of these two wrecks was well pinpointed.

I was especially interested in these two wrecks because unless someone locates a Viking or Phoenician shipwreck someday, these two shipwrecks are the oldest that will ever be found in this hemisphere. Although Columbus had lost other ships during his four voyages, it was always under circumstances that prevented their ever being found.

The two wrecks in St. Anne's Bay were so heavy from the vast amount of water in them that most of their lower sections were pushed deep into the silt and mud. This preserved them from the devastating effects of sea worms, which would have eaten all the wooden parts of the wrecks in a short time. I knew these two wrecks would be of immense interest to historians and archeologists.

On a Sunday in March 1966 my wife, several volunteers and I went to St. Anne's Bay. As we prepared for our first dive, many local residents appeared to warn us that this deep section of the bay was a mating ground for large sharks. They thought we were fools when we laughed off their warning, especially since a fisherman had caught a 14-foot (4.27-meter) tiger shark just the night before.

We swam along in a line, forcing 10-foot-long (3.05 meter) metal rods down into the bottom sediment, trying to locate solid objects that might reveal the presence of a wreck. On our fifth trip we finally struck pay dirt. My wife motioned to me underwater that she needed help. Her rod, which was down about 8 feet (2.44 meters) in the sediment, was stuck in something solid and she couldn't pull it out. We extracted it, and after six hours of excavating by hand, we reached the solid object. It turned out to be a wooden beam.

At first we thought it was only a piling from an old wharf that had sunk in a hurricane in that area over 20 years before, and I ordered everyone to forget about it and continue the search. However, my wife felt that it might be a part of the wreck, and as usual her instinct proved right. Feeling around in the pitch-black hole in the sediment, I discovered that there were treenails, or wooden pegs, in the beam. This was the method by which wood was fastened in the old ships. It was not one used on modern vessels. When we recovered several pieces of obsidian from the hole, I knew that we had made the most important marine archeological discovery to date in the Western Hemisphere. Obsidian is a type of volcanic glass that was found only in Mexico and Central America. Even though darkness was fast approaching, I decided to

make one last dive. I was able to convince only one of my divers, Stan Judge, to join me. We found several more pieces of obsidian, as well as Spanish ceramic shards, or fragments, which also dated from the period of the two wrecks. But before I had decided to call it a day, our dive came to a rather dramatic end: Stan was bitten on the neck by a 2-foot-long (0.61-meter) sea snake, reported to be deadly. In 20 years of diving I had never seen one, nor had I known any other diver who had ever spotted any. We rushed Stan to a hospital, where he was given an injection of serum. A day later he could laugh about the experience.

During the period in which I was awaiting expert confirmation of the nationality and date of the ceramic shards and the origin of the obsidian, we made several more trips to the site and enlarged the hole. We found more ceramic shards and a few ballast stones. The wooden beam certainly appeared to be a ship's beam, but when no other part of the ship was found and we stopped finding artifacts, I decided we had located a small section of one of the Columbus wrecks.

The section must have broken off from the main wrecks, which probably lay close by.

Confirmation finally arrived: the obsidian was from Central America, so Columbus could have brought it with him to St. Anne's Bay; the shards were Spanish and dated from the correct period. I couldn't wait to get back and locate the main sections of the wrecks.

Two years passed before I received governmental approval to search for the main part of the wrecks. In January 1968 Dr. Harold Edgerton of the Massachusetts Institute of Technology came to Jamaica with sonar equipment he had designed especially for locating archeological material buried beneath mud or other sediment. This equipment had already been successful in locating many shipwrecks.

Doc, as Edgerton is called by his friends, was as excited as I about the prospect of discovering these two wrecks. And within an hour of the start of our expedition, we had two positive sonar contacts. From the sonar graphs we knew they were shipwrecks.

Returning to Kingston the following day, I was as happy as if I'd discovered a million dollars in gold. I notified the government of our discoveries and was ordered to organize an expedition to excavate the wrecks. However, I had to refuse to excavate the ships for the time being. There were many things to take into consideration. Because the wrecks were of such great historical importance, I would have to use the most scientific methods of excavation. I had neither the best equipment and personnel nor the funds at the moment to obtain them. Furthermore, I knew that every sliver of wood from these wrecks would be of immense importance, and without a proper preservation laboratory on the island I would end up going down in history as the man who destroyed the Columbus wrecks.

Their wood, once exposed to air, if not properly treated, would disintegrate and be lost forever. I finally convinced the government that we would have to seek financial help from foundations. But I knew that, before any foundation would put up a large amount of money for this project, we would have to establish beyond any doubt that the two wrecks were indeed the Columbus wrecks. We would have to recover a substantial amount of material that could be dated and identified scientifically.

On a project of such importance as this, I decided to enlist the assistance of some of the leading experts in my field. Dr. George Bass of the University of Pennsylvania suggested that we use a coring device to recover sample material. He located one that had been invented by Dr. John Saunders of Columbia University. Saunders not only lent it to us but offered to send one of his assistants to show us how to operate it.

This assistant was Bob Judd, and he turned out to be both a mechanical genius and experienced diver. Back at St. Anne's Bay it took both our strengths to pound the coring tube down into the sediment with a 50-pound (22.68-kilogram) hammer. Extracting it was even more difficult. We finally devised a way for the divers in the skiff to help pull it up with lines. Although the normal underwater visibility was about 20 feet (6.10 meters),

the minute we started pounding the coring tube into the bottom sediment, visibility became nil and the hammer sometimes hit the hands of the diver holding the coring tube rather than the anvil on the top.

Each time we took a sample, it required three hours to pound the coring tube into the sediment, half an hour to pull it out, then another hour to extract the samples delicately from the tube. Everything had to be placed in water-filled jars to prevent drying, and each sample was tagged with the location and depth from which it had been recovered.

Dr. Edgerton's sonar proved its worth. In every single core we found artifacts from the wrecks. By the end of the week we had recovered a piece of Venetian glass, a coral-encrusted tack, a small black bean, several ceramic shards and many fragments of bone, charcoal, wood and ballast stone. On all but one of some 30 cores that were made, the artifacts from the wrecks were recovered from depths of 8 to 10 feet (2.44 to 3.05 meters) beneath the surface of the sea floor. After recovering what I considered a sufficient amount of material for testing, I decided to make a small test hole in the area where we had hit ballast rock and oak wood. This was located at one of the outer extremities of the wreck, at a depth of only 4 feet (1.22 meters) beneath the sea floor. From this small hole, which we later covered over to prevent destruction by sea worms, we recovered about 125 ballast stones of various sizes and a small piece of an oak rib of the ship.

Then the waiting game began, and it turned out to be longer than I had expected. All the datable material we recovered from the site had to be sent to experts in England, Spain and the United States. It took nearly three months until the expected results were in. Most of the ballast stones were found to have come from Central America, the bean was a type grown in Spain, the fragment of glass was dated in the period, as were the ceramic shards. However, when the results of the last test came in, I was at a loss.

This test was the radio carbon-14 dating of the wood. And the wood was dated as 1200 years old. Had I found a Viking ship? I had another test conducted on another sample of wood, and again the same age for the wood was obtained.

After consulting with various dendrologists (tree experts), the mystery was solved. It isn't unknown for an oak tree to live 1000 years, so it is perfectly conceivable that a 700-year-old oak had been cut down and used in building one of the two ships lost by Columbus in St. Anne's Bay.

As a final test of the authenticity of our discovery, I submitted all my findings to the two leading authorities on Columbus—Admiral Samuel Eliot Morison and Mauricio Obregon, a Colombian diplomat and historian. Both agreed that we had found the right wrecks. The search had paid off.

Number of Words: 2434 ÷ _____ Minutes Reading Time = Rate _____

I. SUMMARY

Check √ the seven items listed below that can be included in a
summary of the story.

_____ **1.** Columbus' last voyage   _____ **6.** the wrecks
_____ **2.** the years 1502-04   being found
_____ **3.** Columbus discovering _____ **7.** two wrecks lying
Mexico   in a river
_____ **4.** Columbus sailing   _____ **8.** the historical
for Jamaica   value of the
_____ **5.** two worthless hulks   wrecks being
being left behind   tested
                                     _____ **9.** the find being
                                        confirmed

5 points for each correct answer   SCORE: _____

II. FACT/OPINION

Some of the sentences below express facts. Others state opinions
that may or may not be true. Write F before each sentence that
states a fact and O before each that gives an opinion.

_____ **1.** Columbus' fourth voyage of discovery was his most
dangerous and least profitable one.

_____ **2.** The governor of Santo Domingo disliked Columbus
and delayed sending him aid.

_____ **3.** Indians in the Caribbean liked bells and glass beads
better than food.

_____ **4.** Columbus died of a broken heart, because he had not
been able to find a passage to the Orient.

_____ **5.** The town of New Seville was founded near the spot
where Columbus' wrecked ships lay.

5 points for each correct answer   SCORE: _____

III. SKIMMING

By skimming the story, match the names of the people who helped the author in his search for the wrecks with the places from which they came.

_____ **1.** Dr. Harold Edgerton
_____ **2.** Dr. George Bass
_____ **3.** Sr. Mauricio Obregon

a. University of Pennsylvania
b. Colombia, South America
c. Massachusetts Institute of Technology

5 points for each correct answer   SCORE: _____

IV. GENERALIZATIONS

What can be learned from the story about looking for sunken ships? Check √ the five statements that are generally true.

_____ **1.** Finding old shipwrecks is a very simple task.

_____ **2.** Most old wrecks were lost in circumstances that make finding them impossible.

_____ **3.** Most wooden wrecks have been eaten by worms.

_____ **4.** Some wrecks lie under a layer of sand and sediment.

_____ **5.** Exposing old wrecks to air makes them disintegrate.

_____ **6.** Scientific equipment can aid in finding wrecks.

5 points for each correct answer   SCORE: _____

PERFECT TOTAL SCORE: 100   TOTAL SCORE: _____

V. QUESTIONS FOR THOUGHT

In what ways were the adventures of the author similar to the adventures of Columbus? In what ways were they different?

Detective's Holiday

Octavus Roy Cohen

Hank Granger sought my advice because he heard that I was supposed to know all about hunting and fishing in the sparsely settled country where I lived. Hank was almost 6 feet (1.83 meters) tall and compactly built, and his card informed me that he was a member of the Boston Police Department. From the first I liked him.

He had come quite a distance because he had heard our region was rich in game and fish. "With my annual vacation and accumulated days off, I've got nearly a month—and I'm going to have fun!" he informed me.

He had been unable to get a room at the one small hotel in our village and asked me if there might be a home where he could board. He also wanted to hire a guide who owned a good bird dog. I suggested that he drive with me to Amos Watkins' place.

Amos was a farmer and hunter who knew every inch of the country; he had a comfortable home; a wife and three children, Doug, Pete and Sally; and an assortment of hunting dogs. Since Amos wasn't preoccupied tending his farm at that time of year, he agreed to accommodate Hank as a boarder and act as his guide. Marion Watkins was considerably younger than her husband and obviously devoted to him. She was slim, blonde and pretty—and unmistakably competent. After an enormous lunch I drove Hank Granger back to town to get his luggage.

"Mrs. Watkins doesn't look old enough to be the mother of those children," he said.

"She's not," I explained. "Amos' first wife died several years ago. He met Marion on a trip to the state capital and fell in love with her. At first we all thought it might prove to be a wrong match, but you've never seen such a happy couple."

A client was waiting in my law office, so I asked a friend of mine to take Hank back to Amos'. Hank thanked me profusely and said, "I'm glad you didn't tell them I'm a detective. I'd be pleased if you wouldn't tell anybody. When peaceful folks find out you're a detective, they think you're different from other people, and I'm certainly not."

Several days later I ran into Hank and Amos in the general store, buying supplies. They obviously were getting along fine. When Amos asked me to come out for dinner the following night, I didn't need much urging, for I knew Marion's cooking.

It was an enjoyable evening. Marion played a few simple melodies on an ancient organ, and Amos got out his guitar. But several times during the evening I caught Hank looking at Marion with a steady, searching gaze.

The following Tuesday Amos came to my office, and he looked worried. "Hank's sick," he said. "The doc thinks he's got pneumonia."

I drove out to the Watkins home. If Amos himself had been sick, the household couldn't have been more efficiently adjusted to his needs. Amos had rigged up a buzzer from Hank's bedside to the kitchen. The kids were in the living room playing quietly, their conversation modulated as though they were reluctant to disturb the stranger whom they affectionately called "Uncle Hank."

Doc Stewart was taking care of Hank, administering to his various symptoms, but from the way Marion handled things in the sickroom, I could tell that she had once been a nurse. Amos told me that Hank had insisted on going to the county hospital but that Marion had vetoed the idea. "They're short of nurses. He needs constant attention, and Marion is able to give it to him."

Considering the seriousness of his illness, Hank recovered rapidly. He was granted sick leave to add to his vacation time.

As Hank's convalescence progressed, I sensed a certain tension in the Watkins household. I couldn't explain it, and it worried me. One day, after Hank had recovered enough to take walks around the farm, he said he wanted to have a talk with me. We went to the bench near the spring house and sat.

Hank said, "This is confidential. There's a warrant outstanding for Marion, under her maiden name. The first time I saw her I thought I'd seen her photograph at headquarters, but when I got sick and she nursed me, I knew for sure, because the girl who has been wanted for several years by the police was a nurse, and her description checks."

"What did she do?"

"Two young fellows were caught one evening while they were robbing a store, and she was in their car. She may or may not have been the lookout; anyhow, my duty is to take her back to Boston, but it's a tough decision for me—she pulled me through."

I understood the struggle going on inside the man. I thought of Amos and the three kids and of the warm, happy home Marion had made for them. "Does Marion know that you know?"

"We haven't spoken about it, but I'm sure she does."

I said, "The warrant is under another name; you could be wrong."

"No, a trained detective sees a photograph and it sticks in his mind. It's like something you file away in the drawer, ready to pull out when the time comes."

I said, "You tell me that Marion wasn't actually a participant in the robbery. She was a young girl. Since then she has done all the reforming that any correctional institution could desire, and she's already had her punishment—knowing you suspect her, knowing you might take her back and break up that happy family."

"Don't you suppose I've been over all this a hundred times?" he exclaimed angrily. "Do you think I *want* to hurt Marion and Amos and the kids?" His eruption of anger and frustration departed as suddenly as it had come, and in its stead were misery and bewilderment.

I said, "You're not on duty, you're on vacation."

"A policeman is a policeman twenty-four hours a day. Noth-

ing relieves you from your duty." I decided not to argue any more. This was Hank Granger's problem, and the answer had to be Hank's. I left him and drove home.

Long, anxious days passed, days that seemed interminable, during which I hoped that Hank would see that white was not always white nor black always totally black. Time was running out: his decision could not be postponed indefinitely.

There came a Saturday morning, ugly and sulking with the portent of storm when Amos phoned and asked me to come out that afternoon. They wanted to have an important talk with me. I reached the Watkins house shortly after four o'clock in the midst of a windstorm. Hank and Amos and Marion ushered me into the living room, and the children were sent to their playroom upstairs. The rain came then—a torrential downpour that pounded on the roof and against the windows. Amos said to me, "I wanted you in on this. Hank says he's already discussed the matter with you." I nodded.

"Before Marion consented to marry me, she told me about what happened long ago in Boston," Amos continued.

"Last night Hank let us know who he really is. Neither Marion nor I attempted to influence his decision. If Hank wants to take Marion back to Boston, I will go with them and leave the children with neighbors. I want you to know that we understand Hank's position. He must do what he feels is right."

A broken branch, caught up by the gale, smashed against the house. None of us moved; nobody said anything. Marion was looking at the floor, her cheeks drained of color, her expression one of utter misery. Hank stared at his knuckles. He too looked miserable. There seemed to be nothing more to say. And then, suddenly, terrifyingly, came a sound like a thunderclap as a great pine tree beside the house toppled and crashed on the roof. Just above the kids' room there was a rending and ripping of beams and timbers. We all dashed for the stairway.

Doug, Pete and Sally were running toward us, frightened but unhurt. When they reached the foot of the stairs, they stood uncertainly for a moment and then they rushed to Hank Granger. Pete threw his arms around Hank's leg, and Sally and Doug each grabbed one of

Hank's hands. Sally was crying, and Doug and Pete were trying hard not to. Hank picked the little girl up in his arms.

"You're all right now, Sally," he said softly. "Everything is okay."

Sally whimpered, "Uncle Hank, I was so scared!"

"You're not scared now, are you?" said Hank.

Doug answered, "No, you wouldn't let anything hurt us, would you, Uncle Hank?"

"No," the big man answered, "I sure wouldn't." Hank Granger straightened; his eyes, as bright and clear as his conscience, looked straight at Amos. I knew then that Hank had reached his decision.

Amos and Marion were silent. The gratitude they felt could not be put into words. The storm still raged outside, but it seemed less fierce. The ordeal was over. I felt like applauding. I had watched a fine man doing the thing he believed was right.

Number of Words: 1542 ÷ _____ Minutes Reading Time = Rate _____

I. AUTHOR'S PURPOSE

Check ✓ the sentence below that best explains why the author wrote the story.

_____ **1.** To describe the fishing and hunting trips that can be taken near his home.

_____ **2.** To show how an honest, sensitive person can be faced with a very difficult decision.

_____ **3.** To describe how Marion Watkins' training as a nurse saved Hank Granger's life.

15 points for correct answer   SCORE: _____

II. SEQUENCE

Number the events listed below in the order in which they occurred in the story.

_____ **a.** Hank recognized Mrs. Watkins as being wanted by the police.

_____ **b.** Hank stayed at Amos Watkins' house.

_____ **c.** During a storm, the Watkins children were nearly killed by a falling tree.

_____ **d.** Hank wanted to go fishing and hunting during his vacation.

_____ **e.** Hank got sick, and Marion Watkins looked after him.

_____ **f.** Hank decided not to take Marion back to the Boston police.

_____ **g.** The children rushed to Hank for protection.

5 points for each correct answer   SCORE: _____

III. LANGUAGE USAGE

The author uses colorful, descriptive language in the story. Write the letter (a, b or c) for the sentence that matches the meaning of each sentence below.

> **a.** The roof collapsed.
> **b.** He was no longer troubled.
> **c.** The weather was getting worse.

_____ **1.** The morning was ugly with the portent of storm.

_____ **2.** There was a rending of beams and timbers.

_____ **3.** His eyes were as bright and clear as his conscience.

10 points for each correct answer   SCORE: _____

IV. INFERENCES

Check ✓ the four sentences below that can be inferred from the story.

_____ **1.** Hank's favorite hobby was hunting and fishing.

_____ **2.** Hank was a good, well-trained detective.

_____ **3.** Hank was torn between two conflicting emotions.

_____ **4.** Hank fell in love with Marion.

_____ **5.** Hank finally decided not to arrest Marion.

5 points for each correct answer   SCORE: _____

PERFECT TOTAL SCORE: 100   TOTAL SCORE: _____

V. QUESTION FOR THOUGHT

What difficult moral choice have you (or someone you know) had to make? Describe the situation.

"Milking" Cobras for Cures

Ben Funk

As William E. Haast was walking through the woods in New Jersey, a rabbit hopped casually along in front of him. Haast watched amused, until he spotted a rattlesnake coiled in the path ahead. He clapped his hands and shouted, hoping to frighten the rabbit back into the brush, but he was too late. The serpent struck, burying its fangs into one of the rabbit's legs, and the animal was dead in seconds. "It seemed to me then," Haast recalls, "that such a powerful, destructive force—like atomic energy—could be converted to many good uses, if it were properly controlled."

Since then, Haast has developed a method of producing pure, stable snake venom in powdered form, and as a direct result of his work, the medical profession is using a variety of snake venoms and serums in the treatment of an increasing number of human illnesses, from myasthenia gravis (a killing nerve disease) to migraine headaches. But Haast's path from that stricken rabbit in the Jersey woods to his contribution to world medicine was long, frightening and exceedingly dangerous.

One of Haast's first jobs, as an airline flight engineer in the 1940s, gave him a chance to pursue both his fascination with snakes (at 12 he had kept them as pets) and his theories on the value of venom research. His flights took him to India, where cobras kill 20,000 people a year. During these stopovers he talked with experts and added to his snake collection, bringing several back to the United States in his suitcases. Pilots brought him snakes from Africa, Burma and South and Central America. Before long, with the best collection of exotic reptiles in the country, he quit the airline job and built a serpentarium in Miami, Florida, to produce venom for scientific research. At that time, he said, "the only cobra venoms available in America were imported and cost $1,500 an ounce. I wanted to work out a way to produce a standard, dependable, lower-priced venom and open the way to unlimited research."

Since he was short of money, he enlisted tourists to help him finance the project. On the first day he hung up a sign, 200 people paid 50 cents each to watch him handle his cobras and extract venom from them. Today, in the completed serpentarium, large circular walls enclose landscaped pits in which the reptiles slither through the grass among tropical trees or lie motionless in the shrubbery. Along the outer walls the cobras curl up in air-conditioned compartments. After "milking" the snakes, Haast processes their venom in a spotless laboratory.

In the course of his hazardous activities, Haast has been bitten 126 times. Knowing that this would happen, he had, early in his work, begun injecting cobra venom into his system to build immunity. First, he diluted the venom 1000 times in a saline solution. Gradually, he strengthened the dose. At one point, a zoo curator urged him to stop, pointing out that horses injected with venom to produce snakebite serum had died within two years. But Haast went ahead. Eleven months after he had begun pumping venom into his arms, he was bitten by a cobra. His wife begged him to seek medical aid, but he refused. For several hours he suffered a terrible headache and burning pain around the wound. But he came through all right. In 1949

Technician preparing to extract venom from deadly Siamese cobra

he was nailed by a Mexican moccasin, whose bite can kill a horse in 20 minutes. The venom attacks both the bloodstream and the nervous system. Although the injections of cobra venom had made Haast's nervous system immune to the poison, his blood was as sensitive to the toxin as anyone else's. Fifteen minutes after he was bitten, he began to vomit and reel with spasms of pain. In his record book he noted the time, 6:40 p.m., and his reaction, then collapsed. Mrs. Haast, almost hysterical, tied on a tourniquet, slashed the wound and applied a suction pump to try to draw out the poison, but the spasms grew worse. By 4 a.m. she was certain her husband was dying. Still he refused hospitalization. For four more hours he suffered great torture, but at 8 a.m. the pains receded, and Mrs. Haast was able to write "out of danger" in the record.

Haast subsequently came even closer to death. As usual, he had propped up the glass front door of the compartment of a big Siamese cobra and prepared to take the snake out for venom extraction. To a small group of visitors watching him, it was a moment filled with dread. The reptile reared into

Haast in "shadowboxing" maneuver, while reptile's "cold, glassy eyes" watch as it waits for a chance to strike

striking position, its hood spread, at the first hint of motion through the glass. Now Haast started shadowboxing the cobra; his right hand darted back and forth, inches from the cobra's head—inches from death. The hissing reptile swayed with the hand, watching with cold, glassy eyes for a chance to strike. Haast's strategy was to feint with his right hand, then seize the snake at the back of the head with his left. But this cobra had him figured. In the same split second that Haast's left hand shot in for the capture, the cobra slashed downward at the right forearm. It shot enough venom into Haast's bloodstream to kill 20 humans.

After pulling the cobra's fangs out of his arm, Haast went on with the venom extraction. He then returned the snake to its compartment and finally looked to his wound. It was the worst he had ever received, but he did nothing except wash away the blood. He was not afraid, because he had lived through two other cobra bites in the preceding months.

This time, however, things began to go wrong—and fast. Within minutes his throat was sore, his eyes heavy. Breathing became difficult. A growing weakness crept into his legs. An hour later, when it was time for more extractions, he told his wife, Clarita: "I don't know if I can do it." He was seeing double now, and only by a great effort could he hold his eyelids open. He managed one more extraction, then headed back toward his office.

"He walked like a drunken man," his wife says. "His legs were buckling and I thought he was going to fall. I got him into bed and he began chilling violently. In the next minutes his legs became paralyzed, and he couldn't speak or open his eyes."

This time Haast agreed to call for medical aid. Paralysis was slowly enveloping his throat and lungs, and breathing was becoming almost impossible. By the time his son, Bill Jr., got him to a hospital, Haast was totally paralyzed, as rigid as a board. By the time he was put in an iron lung, breathing had stopped: death had appeared. His face was black, and he felt "as though my mind had separated from my body. It semed that I was standing off to one side and seeing everything that happened. Just before that, I had been fighting for breath like a drowning person. Then a great wave of relief swept over me. I think that is the feeling of death."

But in the iron lung, he began to breathe again. The nurses pried open his jaws and put a suction tube in his mouth to draw out the gathering saliva. For the next 24 hours Haast lay seemingly unconscious. But he was aware of everything done to him and, most of all, of a burning pain as the venom ravaged his system. Very slowly the antibodies in him overcame the effects of the venom. On the second day he could open his eyes. On the third day he could breathe without help. When he was removed from the iron lung, he demanded to be taken home. Two days after his hospital release, he was extracting venom from five king cobras.

Had Haast's body, in fighting off the effects of the two earlier bites, exhausted its immunity? One doctor believed this to be the case and warned him that he had probably developed such a sensitivity to venom that another bite would kill him quickly. But Haast ignored the warning: "There's too much to be done with snake venom. The surface has just been scratched."

A few days later another cobra bit him. "Well," he commented after his recovery, "I guess this knocks the doctor's theory out the window."

Haast first attracted the attention of medical researchers in 1949 when, in rapid succession, he was bitten by two cobras. Again, his wife kept the usual record—paralysis, labored breathing, sporadic heart action, soaring temperature. When it was over, Haast studied the record and told Clarita, "That looks just like polio."

He hurried to the University of Miami research laboratories, advanced his theory, and was invited to participate in an experiment with rhesus monkeys often used in research. Polio virus was injected into all the animals. This was followed immediately by mild shots of detoxified venom in half of the monkeys. The ones who didn't get the venom contracted paralysis and other polio symptoms in the normal time. Those given the venom were not affected until hours later.

What had happened, the researchers said, was that an "interference phenomenon" had been created. Scientists had known for many years of such a phenomenon. A conflict can be created between two infectious agents, so that the victim can survive without infection from either.

The university gave Haast a grant-in-aid and sent him to India to collect more cobras. He was allowed to keep them in his serpentarium. In return, he supplied the university with venom at a low price. The experiments continued, and out of them came exciting promise of a polio cure—just before the Salk vaccine came onto the scene.

Since then, medical laboratories here and abroad have

been pursuing research in the use of venom, with increasingly impressive results. "Venoms have powerful physiological properties," says Dr. Daniel Drachman of John Hopkins University in Baltimore. "Bill Haast realized that long before scientists did. He foresaw its effects and inspired the opening of a new field in research of the nervous system."

Dr. Murray Sanders, head of the Sanders Medical Research Foundation in Boca Raton, Florida, uses venoms to treat "Lou Gehrig's disease," an ailment so-called because it took the life of the famed "iron man" of the New York Yankees. A relentless destroyer of the central nervous system, the malady has baffled the medical world.

Sanders had been a member of the University of Miami team that did the successful venom experiments in polio treatment. Because the symptoms of polio and "Lou Gehrig's disease" are similar, he began to test the effect of venom on animals suffering from the latter disease. The results were rewarding. So Sanders, using a mixture of cobra venom and another snake venom, began to treat human victims of the disease. He has treated more than

800. Some who came to him paralyzed and helpless are walking again and partially able to take care of themselves. A cure for this terrible disease remains elusive. But Sanders says, "The backbone of research in this field is the source of venom. Bill Haast has provided it, and God knows he has paid the price."

Dr. John H. Laragh of the Cornell Medical Center in New York is using cobra venom to treat patients with high blood pressure, and he says the results have been "extremely promising." At the Howard Hughes Medical Research Foundation in Miami, Dr. Robert A. Nelson discovered that a nontoxic cobra-venom factor prevents rejections of transplants in animals. In Mexico City, Dr. Caroline Molinari reported encouraging results in the use of Haast's venoms in treatment of both animal and human cancers.

The effectiveness of venom, particularly in the treatment of diseases of the nervous system, seems somewhat surprising, for venom attacks the motor nerve endings, thereby blocking the impulses that govern muscular function. This causes rapid paralysis, hence respiratory failure—and death. But when the venoms are broken down and the toxic elements are removed, the opposite happens. The purified venom fractions go to work to repair the damaged nerve endings from which impulses are translated from one nerve to the other. This impedes the nerve destruction that occurs in Lou Gehrig's disease and many other afflictions. Since nerves affected by stress are also at the root of such ailments as high blood pressure, venom is helpful in treating those conditions.

Haast has received wide recognition for his work, as well as numerous awards and citations "for unusual service to humanity" and "for heroic contributions to the saving of lives by offering himself as a human guinea pig."

By now, Haast's blood is so full of venom antibodies that it has become a perfect serum for snakebite victims. He has given it freely and has saved the lives of 22 people. He has flown on a

After "milking" the snake, Haast processes its venom for research in various human diseases.

moment's notice to hospitals far from his home in order to donate his blood, which he gives free of charge while footing the bill for his trip.

For a man who has done so much to save lives, one recent event has been devastating. It occurred when a visitor to the serpentarium perched his 6-year-old son on the wall of a circular pit that was the home of an African Nile crocodile. When the father turned away for a moment, the boy toppled into the pit and was instantly killed by the beast. It was the only such tragedy that had ever occurred at the serpentarium and Haast was heartbroken. He killed the crocodile, which took 24 shots from a Luger, and buried it on the spot. His grief was so intense that he decided to close the serpentarium and abandon his life's work. But the boy's mother called and urged him to continue. Her family, she said, revered him for his work and did not want him to abandon it because of an accident that was not his fault.

So Haast is once again at his absorbing and perilous work. He has flirted with death so many times he is sure he knows exactly what it will be like to die if one of his serpents finally kills him. But the pain and the convulsive struggle for life have only strengthened his dedication.

"It's a good feeling to know that I've saved some lives and prevented a lot of suffering," he says. "It's worth all the days of torture. A person should never fear death. I've got much to live for, but I wouldn't be afraid to die. I think I know that when a man dies, the experience isn't a bad one. The feeling is one of great relief, like a badly beaten fighter gets when the bell finally ends that last round."

Number of Words: 2474 ÷ _____ Minutes Reading Time = Rate _____

I. SUPPORTING DETAILS

Circle the letter (a, b or c) before the answer that best completes each of the sentences below.

1. Haast's work with venomous snakes has been of use to _____.
   a. dentistry   **b.** tourism   **c.** medicine

2. The first study that used Haast's ideas about venom dealt with _____.
   a. polio   **b.** migraine   **c.** cancer

3. Venoms are being used in the treatment of diseases of the _____.
   a. nervous system   **b.** kidneys   **c.** blood vessels

4. The venom of the Mexican moccasin attacks both the nervous system and the _____.
   a. ears   **b.** digestive system   **c.** blood

5 points for each correct answer   SCORE: _____

II. CAUSE/EFFECT

Match each cause listed below to its effect. Write the letter (a, b, c or d) for an effect (column B) before its cause (column A).

A	B
____ **1.** Because Haast can produce pure, stable venom powder	**a.** his blood is the perfect snakebite serum.
____ **2.** Because he has built a large serpentorium	**b.** it is being used to treat many illnesses.
____ **3.** Because he has often been bitten by snakes	**c.** his heroic contribution was recognized.
____ **4.** Because his work brought him close to death	**d.** snakes can be "milked" of their venom.

10 points for each correct answer   SCORE: _____

III. PROBLEM SOLVING

The story mentions a number of ways Haast has dealt with deadly snake bites. Circle the letter (a, b or c) for the answer that describes each of these ways.

1. To build immunity in his system, he
   a. let himself be bitten by small snakes.
   b. began injecting himself with diluted venom.
   c. swallowed special antivenom pills.

2. When he was bitten by a snake, his wife
   a. tied on a tourniquet and tried to suck out the poison.
   b. killed the snake.
   c. pulled the fangs out of his arms.

3. After a particularly serious cobra bite, he
   a. began screaming in pain.
   b. was put in an iron lung to help him breathe.
   c. lost his sense of hearing.

4. When other people were bitten by snakes, he
   a. gave them a special antitoxin in powdered form.
   b. studied their reactions: paralysis, fever, etc.
   c. gave his own blood as an antivenom serum.

10 points for each correct answer   SCORE: _____

PERFECT TOTAL SCORE: 100   TOTAL SCORE: _____

IV. QUESTION FOR THOUGHT

Why do you think so many people are more afraid of snakes than of almost anything else? Explain your reasons.

Lone Star Attraction

Mary Lynn Kotz

Keynote speaker, Representative Barbara Jordan, acknowledging audience of delegates at a Democratic National Convention

"Even as a child, she was one of the rare ones," Barbara Jordan's father once said.

They're still saying that about the tall, earnest black woman from Texas, who is one of the most admired women in the country. By her late thirties she had served in the U.S. House of Representatives, had been awarded honorary degrees by 24 universities, among them Harvard and Notre Dame, and had been singled out for honors and awards by more than 200 national organizations.

She says of all the attention, "I'm just delighted," and grins disarmingly. Yet it is typical of her that, when her career in

69

the House of Representatives seemed assured for as long as she would wish, she suddenly announced that she wasn't seeking reelection. It was a bold and, some say, courageous step—to face political reality and then to seize her own options.

Barbara Jordan first stirred a national television audience on July 25, 1974. The House Judiciary Committee was holding hearings on the impeachment of the President of the United States. Listening to that ringing voice say, "My faith in the Constitution is whole, it is complete, it is total," you *knew* that the matter was being considered most seriously, with honest intent.

Two years later, again before a television audience, she lifted spirits with her keynote speech at the Democratic National Convention. "I feel that, notwithstanding the past, my presence here is one additional bit of evidence that the American Dream need not forever be deferred."

Barbara Jordan clearly is one who has overcome. Propelled by her dynamic speaking ability and her commanding presence, this proud product of a Houston ghetto has catapulted to national prominence in a very brief period. However, she does not depend upon being black, or a woman.

"I am a politician," she insists, "a professional politician. I didn't get here by being black or a woman. I got here by working hard. My life is my work."

Barbara Jordan remains something of a mystery. She is not a joiner. In Washington she lives alone in her apartment. In Houston she shares the small frame home of her childhood with her widowed mother. She is stern and decisive, with a razor-sharp way of dealing with foolishness. She says "no" more often than "yes" and can turn you to ice with a look. Yet she is also compassionate and warm. Indeed, her warmth is extraordinary: when it is focused upon you, you sense a great *caring* spirit.

Yes, there seem to be two Barbara Jordans. One is the powerful and effective legislator with an incisive, legal mind, who has pared away the nonessentials until her life runs like a well-managed machine.

The other is the warm, fun-loving friend who can laugh her way through a stuffy party and move a roomful of people to silence when she plays her guitar and sings spirituals.

One key to Barbara Jordan is her ability to concentrate her energies on one thing at a time. "Unless you develop the capacity to focus in a singular way, you find yourself focusing on nothing—not being very adept or expert in anything," she says. "You must have an area of interest and develop maximum knowledge in that area in order to be productive and successful."

Barbara Jordan's area of interest is, of course, the law and its political adaptation. Her great heroes are Thomas Jefferson and John Marshall. Her goals, to which she is deeply committed, are to achieve individual freedom, equality and openness of government.

Everyday, from 8:45 a.m., when she walks into her office with a cheerful "Greetings!" for her staff, until 9 p.m. when she goes home, a bundle of papers under her arm for evening study, she wrestles with the complexities of law and lawmaking.

She has streamlined every aspect of her life and has little time for interests other than work. She has chosen a path that does not include the time, energy and emotion that other women devote to a husband and children. "Politics is al-most totally consuming," she has said. "A good marriage requires that one attend to it and not treat it as a hobby."

Often, she wishes that she could do more of the things she enjoys, like listening to music, singing or chatting with friends. But, in the final balance, she feels that her "singular focus" is worth the time and energy she puts into it.

Though Barbara Jordan is a national figure, the people in her district, their needs and their problems, consume her life. She responds with compassion to their individual troubles as if the people were members of her own family.

One Saturday she was shopping for clothes in a Houston department store. A young woman, a stranger, rushed up to her and said, "Please help me. I've been out of work for six months, and I can't get any aid from the state." Barbara Jordan listened to her desperate story, then called the state employment director herself to help the woman get a job.

She goes home twice a month to meet with people, to speak, to be with her mother and sisters, to sing in the choir at the Good Hope Baptist Church. "My roots are in Texas. My family have been Texans as long as anybody remembers," she says. "My grandfather, Charles Jordan, was able to buy our home there with help from Roosevelt's New Deal. We never knew we were poor, but we knew we were Texans."

Barbara Charlene Jordan, third and youngest daughter of a Baptist minister, was early recognized as gifted and encouraged by her family and teachers to pursue those gifts.

"I'm behind you, as far as you want to go," said her father. He stressed education as the tool to surmount the obstacles to a poor, black child in a segregated city. Her parents taught her to demand the best from herself. If she were capable of A's, she should not be satisfied with B's.

The family was close-knit, with a strong, fundamentalist religion. Her parents poured almost all their energies into raising their three talented daughters.

"They were hardworking, caring people—caring for their family," Barbara Jordan recalled. "My father always worked as a laborer in a warehouse. My mother was a good housewife and a good mother, and she was always available to my sisters and me."

Barbara and her sisters, Benny and Rose Mary, sang in the choir, studied Scripture and longed for the dances, the movies, the teenage fun that their religion prohibited. But they respected the prohibitions. Her sisters went off to college to major in music. Their parents expected Barbara to follow in their footsteps. But Barbara had other ideas. She had thought first of going into science. But when a black lawyer, Edith Sampson, made a dramatic "career day" speech at her high school, Barbara decided she wanted to be a lawyer.

In 1952 in the South such an idea was radical, but Barbara was determined.

She entered Texas Southern, a small black university in Houston, and immediately ran for president of her class. (She lost.) She got involved in competitive debate, an activity that consumed her for the next four years. Her strong, resonant voice was a natural gift. Her diction was a gift from her father, who taught her precise, accent-less English almost syllable by syllable. Debating polished those gifts and carried her outside Texas. The debate team visited colleges in the

North, won many championships, even tied Harvard. She developed poise under fire.

She graduated *magna cum laude* (with great distinction) from TSU in 1956 and entered Boston University Law School as a "first and only"—woman and black—a role she would play many times over. While she was in law school, another young Boston University graduate, Dr. Martin Luther King, Jr., opened the curtain of the civil rights movement. Barbara was touched by the notion that she, too, might be able to change the way Southern laws excluded her people.

Her way of making things better was through politics. She came home with her law degree in 1960, set up practice on her mother's dining-room table and went to work in her neighborhood for the Kennedy-Johnson campaign. Her speechmaking impressed local politicians. In 1962 she ran for the Texas legislature. She lost. In 1964 she ran again and lost again. Then, in 1966, in a new, predominantly black and Mexican-American district created by the Supreme Court's one-person one-vote rule, she won a seat in the Texas Senate—the first black senator in a century. She served for six years, carving out a reputation for honesty, intellect and political knowledge. She made allies of the state's white politicians, up to and including President Johnson.

He adopted her—some say, as his only political heir. He taught her his own political skills, appointed her to a national advisory committee and brought her to the White House. He urged her to run for Congress in 1972 and campaigned for her. When she was elected by an overwhelming majority, he helped her get on the Judiciary Committee.

Sharing platform with Presidential nominee Jimmy Carter and the late Hubert Humphrey, Barbara Jordan enjoys convention spotlight.

The secret of her success has been that same old ability to focus. Her issues have been those closest to her heart—those giving ordinary citizens a chance at the same opportunities she forged for herself.

The work of which she is proudest includes laws that ensure the right to vote for Spanish-speaking Americans, protect consumers against price-fixing and guarantee hospital patients the right to an itemized bill. She has affixed her name to 31 new laws or amendments. One that did not pass, but which she still supports wholeheartedly, guarantees Social Security benefits to homemakers.

What is next for Barbara Jordan now that she has decided to give up her safe seat in the House? As usual, she is keeping her own counsel.

But whatever way she goes, you can be sure that Barbara Jordan will focus her considerable energy and intellect just as sharply on the next phase of her life.

Number of Words: 1683 ÷ _____ Minutes Reading Time = Rate _____

I. SKIMMING

By skimming the story, match some of the important events in Barbara Jordan's life listed below (column A) with the years in which they occurred (column B). Write the letter (a, b, c, d, e or f) for each date in its correct place.

	A	B
_____ **1.**	entered Texas Southern	**a.** 1962
_____ **2.**	entered Boston University	**b.** 1972
_____ **3.**	lost her first race in Texas	**c.** 1974
_____ **4.**	was elected to the Texas Senate	**d.** 1952
_____ **5.**	was elected to Congress	**e.** 1966
_____ **6.**	drew national attention on TV	**f.** 1956

5 points for each correct answer   SCORE: _____

II. CHARACTERIZATION

Check √ the four statements that describe Barbara Jordan's character, as presented in the story.

_____ **1.** She is a boisterous person, enjoys going to loud parties and working in a noisy office.

_____ **2.** She has a sharp mind and is able to concentrate her energies on the problem at hand.

_____ **3.** She devotes most of her life to her work.

_____ **4.** She is not afraid to tackle new careers.

_____ **5.** She is committed to her political goals, which include giving ordinary citizens equal opportunities.

_____ **6.** She is easily discouraged by failure.

5 points for each correct answer   SCORE: _____

III. MAIN IDEA

Check ✓ the one sentence that best describes what the story is about.

_____ 1.   Barbara Jordan, the hard working congresswoman from Texas, is much-admired.

_____ 2.   Congresswoman Barbara Jordan is working hard to become a judge.

_____ 3.   Barbara Jordan grew up to be the first black woman to enter Boston University Law School.

20 points for correct answer   SCORE: _____

IV. CRITICAL THINKING

Circle the letter (a, b or c) for the correct answer to each question.

1.   What kind of story did the author write?
     a. a biased report   **b.** a factual report
                         c. an overblown tribute

2.   What kind of portrait does the author draw of Ms. Jordan?
     a. insulting   **b.** one-sided   **c.** realistic

3.   How does Ms. Jordan emerge from the story?
     a. a larger-than-life heroine
     b. a dynamic, committed person
     c. an indecisive person, unable to settle on a career

10 points for each correct answer   SCORE: _____

PERFECT TOTAL SCORE: 100   TOTAL SCORE: _____

V. QUESTION FOR THOUGHT

Which of Barbara Jordan's achievements do you admire the most? Explain your reasons.

On a clear warm December day in 1967 the water over Metis Shoal suddenly began to change color. The coral shoal is near the Tonga Islands, a scattered cluster of landfalls 1800 miles (2898 kilometers) this side of Australia, and the Pacific there is usually deep blue. But on that particular day it turned a sickly green and yellow, the water cloudy with mud. As one day became two and two became a week, the water began to churn and bubble. By the morning of December 11, the smoke and steam rising 6000 feet (9660 kilometers) into the air could be seen for 70 miles (112.7 kilometers), leading to reports from native fishermen that the world was coming to an end.

Instead of an end, it was a beginning. By sundown an incandescent island—a half mile

Long Live the Center for Short-Lived Phenomena!

Skip Rozin

77

(2.4 kilometers) long, 150 feet (45 meters) high and glowing cherry red—had pushed its way to the surface where a day before only water had been. The island's creator was a volcanic eruption, loud and violent, ejecting molten lava and rocks in great arcs to a height of 1000 feet (300 meters). Within two weeks the volcano had built a kidney-shaped island 4 miles (6.4 kilometers) long.

While not unknown, such undersea volcanoes are rare. And the islands produced by their eruptions contain information about the nature of the earth and how it works that is not found anywhere else. But these eruptions tend to occur in isolated places, so that scientists are seldom aware of what is happening. Furthermore, islands formed in such a catastrophic way have a habit of slipping back into the sea before anyone has noticed they ever existed.

The island at Metis Shoal was like that. Fifty-eight days after pushing its way to the surface, attended by neither noise nor fireworks, it slid back into the ocean.

But not unnoticed. Before it sank, a complete scientific investigation was made. Photographs—taken by a variety of passing planes and boats during its eight-week life—were collected and edited, and a scientist actually reached the island to collect rock and lava samples for analysis. For the first time, the birth and death of a volcanic island—one of the great mysteries of the earth— was recorded with scientific precision.

This achievement verified the efficiency of an early-warning system called the Center for Short-Lived Phenomena. Located at the Smithsonian Astrophysical Observatory in Cambridge, Massachusetts, the Center is a sort of news service for the international science community. On a 24-hour-a-day basis it receives reports of events happening all over the world, then relays the information to interested scientists for further examination and interpretation. The main stipulation is simply that the event, like the eruption of the island at Metis Shoal, should be in the process of happening or have just happened.

With a full-time staff of only five people, the Center reported more than 500 events in the first five years since its creation by the Smithsonian Institution. The appearance of a floating island in the Caribbean, the impact of a meteorite in Connecticut, the death of 10,000 robins in a potato field in southern Florida—such things normally get a few paragraphs' mention in some local newspaper. To the Center and its knowing clients, they may be crucial news.

The Center itself is not very impressive—six small offices, painted an institutional light green and furnished with military-surplus desks and big gray file cabinets stuffed with records and reports that long ago overflowed onto the desks and chairs and floors.

"It is the short-lived events in nature that tell you the most about natural systems," explains Bob Citron, director of the Center. "Nothing can tell a geologist more about the fundamental earth processes than an earthquake or a volcanic eruption, but he or she has got to go in there and observe them while they're happening.

"Speed," he says, leaning forward over his cluttered desk, "is the crucial element. To astrophysicists, a freshly fallen meteorite may be priceless. Let it sit for five or six days, and it becomes a museum piece, practically worthless in the laboratory."

Since speed is the Center's most important commodity, it is not by chance that it is located on the top floor of the Smithsonian Astrophysical Observatory. Below is the observatory's communications room crammed with humming, idling machines: six teletype circuits—including Western Union domestic and international, ITT and RCA international, NASA and the institute's satellite-tracking networks—and nine telephone lines.

The Center's global sensors include 2300 corresponding scientists and scientific stations in 148 countries, working mostly under informal agreements in a mutual-aid network. Each scientist covers his or her geographic area for the Center and in return receives immediate reports of all events in his or her particular discipline from all over the world.

Whatever the event, the Center's procedure varies little. It always starts with a correspondent somewhere noticing something out of the ordinary. It does not have to be something spectacular, and often its true importance is not realized until much later.

In mid-September 1968 a few reports began to come in to the Center concerning migrating squirrels in the southeastern part of the United States. Nothing alarming, just an increase in the number of gray squirrels seen on roads and in yards. On receiving the first alert, the Center notified every interested scientist, agency and institution with "fast response" capabilities. Then an Event Notification Card was sent to each subscriber. The cards give complete information on an event. This includes where and when it took place, what happened and the name and address of the source of the news.

As additional reports of the migration came in, the Center issued successive Event Infor-mation Cards, one for each change in the migration's status. And the status did change as reports came in from North and South Carolina, Tennessee, Kentucky, Georgia, Alabama, New York, Pennsylvania and Massachusetts. They showed that the "eruption" involved possibly as many as 20 million animals, moving independently and in every direction imaginable, and that tens of thousands were starving, dying on highways and drowning in their attempts to swim across lakes and reservoirs.

During the four weeks of peak squirrel activity, the Center stayed in touch with 71

biologists, mammologists and research institutions, and it distributed daily information reports to 121 biological correspondents around the world.

Early explanations for the massive migration centered on a bumper crop the preceding year that produced two highly successful breeding seasons. That took care of the number of squirrels but not their odd behavior. It was only later, when scientists could pool their findings and check records of similar phenomena, that the cause was linked to the natural habits of the gray squirrel. Unlike its cousins, which store food in hollow trees, the gray squirrel tucks nuts and seeds under leaves or a little dirt. Each fall he "reshuffles" his stores, collecting old nuts and hiding them in new places, in the process moving farther and farther away from familiar grounds. The increased number of squirrels pressed him still farther, so far that many became "confused and disoriented" and responded by migrating even farther.

Biologists came away from the study concluding that the conditions contributing to the event were not so rare and that additional migrations might be expected, probably of a similar

nature and at the same time of year.

As the case of the Appalachian Squirrel Migration indicates, the Center works simply to collect information and get it as quickly as possible to where it will be of the most value. Though it has no investigative powers of its own, the center does initiate follow-up studies by its correspondents. As a result, four of every five events reported are fully investigated.

"A biologist can study squirrel habits and life-styles all his or her life," says Citron, "but nothing can give more insight than to have something happen abruptly like a population explosion or a major migration. It can add a whole new dimension to looking at one's subject."

Each event the Center covers is classified according to its character into one of four divisions: earth science, astrophysics, urgent anthropology and biological science. The first includes volcanic eruptions, avalanches and earthquakes. The second includes meteorite falls and meteors (a meteorite is a meteor until it strikes the earth), and the third is for events like the discovery in 1970 of the Guajaka, the Stone Age tribe of Indians located in Paraguay. Such events are considered short-lived because whatever scientific value they have is threatened by contamination by civilization. The fourth division includes oil spills, insect infestations and unusual animal activity like the squirrel migration.

The original idea for the Center came from Dr. Sidney Galler, who recognized the need for an early-alert system when he was head of biological research for the Navy. In 1965, having become the Smithsonian's assistant secretary for science, Galler drew up plans for such a system, using the existing communications for the satellite-tracking network of the Institution's Astrophysical Observatory. The Center moved in upstairs with Bob Citron as its director and sole employee. Until then, Citron had supervised the Smithsonian's satellite-tracking stations in Africa.

"In the beginning I had a little office downstairs, a telephone and a typewriter," says Citron, who, in addition to being an expert in monitoring systems, is a professional photographer.

Within weeks, he received word of the activity at Metis Shoal and began immediately to contact ships and planes in the area for eyewitness accounts. Some of them obligingly made detours to collect data and photographs. Citron also got a Smithsonian scientist, Dr. Charles Lunkquist, who was on his way to Australia, to divert to the site, take pictures, collect samples and send back "real-time" reports.

"I dispersed the information to volcano centers all over the world," says Citron, "and people said, 'Hey, this is really working.' News spread by word of mouth, and soon everybody said if you want news about volcanoes, contact the Center."

From such informal beginnings, the Center's activities have grown in range, prestige and usefulness. Of its new projects, none is more ambitious nor more important to the Center than Earthwatch. This is a global monitoring and research network that Citron has been planning with the United Nations. The plan was approved at the Stockholm Human Environment Conference in June 1972. Now it needs only final approval and funding by the U.N. To the Center, it will mean a sharp rise in the number of events covered each year. In a sense it will bring

environmental awareness to places totally isolated from the realities of world ecology.

The difference between the Center's activities and Earthwatch is fundamental: the Center's mission is to observe and report; Earthwatch's will be to act as an early-alert system and to take that information and use it to assess all facets of the world environment and make suggestions for changes. Or, as Citron puts it, to "take a holistic view of earth management."

As the nucleus of the alert system, the Center will help gather the data on which the other divisions of Earthwatch can act. It will form links with other monitoring networks around the earth—33 major and thousands of minor programs concerned with different aspects of the environment. The Center plans to enlist the aid of science classes in thousands of universities and secondary schools all over the world. Biology classes studying the environment in their own areas will act as the first line of observers. If the plans work, students will turn in their findings to their teachers, who will send those important enough to a national coordinator, a professional scientist acting as a filter. Investigating teams will then be assigned to events requiring further study. By making use of existing systems, the Center's plan recalls the way the first post offices in frontier America were located in the already established general stores.

"We are right on the frontiers of man's knowledge of this planet," says Citron. "In order to keep track of what's going on, to try and understand the very fundamental nature of what goes on in the earth, on the earth, and in the biosphere, we have to keep our fingers on the pulse of the planet."

He envisions the Center as a vast storehouse of information. It would be catalogued and cross-referenced so that an animal migration in the eastern United States is not an isolated event but can be compared with events in other places over a century-long period.

"A hundred years from now anyone will be able to come to our archives and study almost everything that has happened to the planet from 1968 on," he says. "We'll be able to see changes in the planet and, for the first time, to make an assessment of our impact on the globe."

Number of Words: 2163 ÷ _____ Minutes Reading Time = Rate _____

I. CLASSIFYING

The Center for Short-Lived Phenomena classifies events into four categories. Two of these are earth science and biological science. Indicate which of the categories the events listed below belong to by placing a check √ in the correct column.

		Earth Science	Biological Science
1.	a volcanic eruption	___	___
2.	a migration of squirrels	___	___
3.	a plague of mice	___	___
4.	an earthquake	___	___
5.	an avalanche	___	___
6.	an infestation of snails	___	___

5 points for each correct answer   SCORE: _____

II. GENERALIZATIONS

From the story, what can be learned about natural phenomena? Check √ the four statements below that are generally true.

_____ **1.** Many events of scientific importance can occur without scientists being aware of them.

_____ **2.** Many natural events lose their scientific value if they are not studied as quickly as possible.

_____ **3.** Scientists can always learn more by studying nature directly than by working in a laboratory.

_____ **4.** Some natural events cannot be explained or understood unless complete information about them is available.

_____ **5.** Short-lived phenomena add to our knowledge of science.

5 points for each correct answer   SCORE: _____

III. OUTLINING

Complete the outline of the story below by writing the letter (a, b, c, d or e) for each of the following sentences in its proper place.

> **a.** The Center is expanding its activities to include Earthwatch.
> **b.** There was a volcanic eruption.
> **c.** The Center receives information from over 2,000 scientists.
> **d.** Scientists were able to study the eruption in detail.
> **e.** In this way, events can be studied immediately.

I. In December 1967, a strange event occurred near the Tonga Islands.
   A. _____
   B. A new island appeared out of the ocean.
   C. A few weeks later, it sank back beneath the water.
   D. _____
II. The Center for Short-Lived Phenomena was formed to inform scientists of events happening around the world.
   A. _____
   B. The Center passes the information on to other scientists.
   C. _____
III. _____

10 points for each correct answer   SCORE: _____

PERFECT TOTAL SCORE: 100   TOTAL SCORE: _____

IV. QUESTION FOR THOUGHT

How would you know if something that happened around you was a "Short-Lived Phenomenon" worthy of scientific study? Explain the reasons that would help you decide.

The Real American Cowboy

William H. Forbis

He had an heroic image of himself as a hard-riding, fast-shooting hombre, and that is how he appears in books and paintings of the Old West. It is true that most cowboys did break wild horses. And some did in fact shoot it out with Indians or lasso bears.

The real American cowboy, however, was more often a dirty, overworked laborer who fried his brains under a prairie sun or rode endless miles in rain and wind to shepherd the unlovable, thick-headed, panic-prone creatures that gave him his name.

His great years lasted a bare generation, from the end of the Civil War until the mid-1880s. Then bad weather, poor range management, the introduction of barbed wire and declining prices for beef forced an end to the old freewheeling ways of long drives from range to market. In that brief span the number of cowboys who rode the cattle trails across the Great Plains totaled no more than 40,000, with the average cowpuncher riding the range for only seven years before settling for good in town or on his own ranch.

All sorts of people became cowhands. Most were surprisingly young (their average age was 24). Many were Mexican, Indian or black. A number were mustered-out Union or Confederate soldiers. The cowboy's educational level was reflected in the remark of one Texas-born lad: "Well, when I got so I could draw a cow and mark a few brands on the slate, I figured I was getting too smart to stay in school."

The basic ingredient of the cowboy's function and identity was the horse. Few cowboys actually owned a horse—their mounts were supplied by the ranch they worked for. The relationship between man and horse was a practical arrangement, rather than the love affair, familiar to us from Westerns, between a kindly master and a faithful servant. Most cowboys were resolute in their judgment that "a man afoot is no man at all." As cowpuncher Jo Mora put it, the dismounted cowboy was "just a plain bowlegged human who smelled horsy at times, slept in his underwear and was subject to boils."

Another proud possession was a gun. Cowboys were aware of the tough air that guns gave them, and they weighed themselves down with firearms whenever they paid a call on a girl, confident that she would be impressed. But in trying to appear manly, more than one cowboy managed to look just plain silly. A Montana man remembered a cowboy relative who returned from town with a bullet wound. Presumably he had received it in a saloon battle. In fact, the poor puncher had shot himself, though not seriously, when a photographer handed him the gun so he could pose looking fierce for the home folks.

HOME ON THE RANGE. The cowboy carried himself with a sort of vinegary pride, fully convinced that he was an aristocrat among the working-men of the West. An Englishman visiting a friend on a ranch in Wyoming discovered this quality when he inquired of the foreman, "Is your master at home?" The foreman looked at him levelly and replied, "The man who's my master hasn't been born yet."

Stoicism was a deeply rooted trait among range hands. Complaining was considered unprofessional. It irritated others and evoked no sympathy whatever. But few careers have ever offered more occasions for complaint. On a given day a cowboy could find himself in the middle of quicksand, a prairie fire or a stampede; he could be thrown or kicked by a horse; charged by a cow or half frozen by a winter search for strayed livestock. Exposure to the extremes of the weather frequently brought on pneumonia, which, along with riding accidents, was a leading cause of cowboy deaths.

The most reverent feelings of cowboys in this Victorian time were reserved for women. It was a remote reverence. Marriage was a mode of life that most cowboys had to shun, since they were always on the move and their pay was too low to support a family. But all the while they rode the trails, they yearned for the company of women. A lonesome young cowboy would travel miles, by one account, "just to sit on a porch for an hour or two and watch some homesteader's red-faced daughter rock her chair and scratch her elbows."

The bunkhouse was little more than a rural slum. Typically, it was a shack made from weatherboard or cottonwood logs. Whatever the design, there was one constant that made bunkhouses instantly recognizable: the smell. The aroma that hit the senses of anyone walking in was a mixture of sweaty men, dry cow manure, the licorice in chewing-tobacco plugs, old work boots and the smoke from coal-oil or tallow lamps. There was a uniform look to these places, too, a chronic state of untidiness. Clothes were "hung on the floor," as one historian of the cowboy era said, "so they wouldn't fall down and get lost."

Despite discomfort and boredom, cowboys managed to accept the raw-edged routine of bunkhouse life and the basic range-land philosophy that underlay it. For every cowhand was aware that a ranch was set up for the care and well-being of cows, not people. When he was not killing time around the bunkhouse, he knew that he would be spending most of his hours and months tending cattle or enduring dozens of other dirty or monotonous chores that bore little resemblance to any glamorized vision of cowboy life.

TOIL AND TROUBLE. The long drive was the grandest and most grueling adventure that cowboy life offered. It was the climactic event of the cowboy's working life, the chance to prove his strength and ability by chasing great herds of longhorns from the home range, where they were worth $4, to a point of sale, where they might bring $50 a head.

Whether the size of the herd was 500 or 2500 head, each drive generated its special measure of toil and trouble. Steers would drown in sinkholes at the river crossings. Settlers drove the herds from their fields with guns. There was rarely enough water for the cattle and never enough sleep for the weary cowhands: on the drive, a puncher might work 18 hours a day seven days a week, and he might travel 1800 miles with no comforts other than a campfire and his bedroll.

Yet the cowboy went eagerly. Never mind that in return for three to four months of dust, thirst, blisters, cold and danger he received a paltry $100 in hard wages—barely the price of a new hat and a pair of fancy boots. There were compensations: the comradeship of the trail, the satisfaction of passing the toughest test in the trade and perhaps, too, a proud awareness of being part of something fundamental and grand. Challenges and emotions such as these, coupled in some cases with the sheer necessity of holding a job, drew cowboys onto the trail.

The greatest danger on the drive was the nighttime stampede. A thousand things could make the cattle rise and run—anything from a cannon shot of prairie thunder to the flare of a match as a cowboy lighted a cigarette. Oddly, when the cattle stampeded, they uttered no sound at all. A sleeping trail hand would suddenly be aware of a deep rumbling, a trembling of sod beneath him. He would know that the cattle were off and running. And as the trail boss bellowed, "All hands and the cook," the crew would run, stumbling through the dark to mount their horses. The longhorns, though angular and ungainly to look at, ran with surprising speed, their hoofs pounding and their horns clashing as they thundered along. In the words of one cowboy, a stampeding herd looked like a "tempest of horns and tails."

Two or three cowboys, usually the best riders, spurred hard to get out in front of the stampede. After three or four terrifying miles, the cattle usually began to circle, then mill. For the hands this was one of the most dangerous times: with the herd jammed tight a trapped horseman might be jostled from his mount and trampled to death.

TRAIL'S END. When the riders on a long drive crested the last rise and in the distance saw the wisps of smoke or the flickering lamps that signaled trail's end, each cowhand felt a surge of almost irrepressible desire. For months the men had bathed only in the muddy waters of river fords and had the look and smell of a summer in the saddle. Now, with the cattle town finally in sight, each man knew what he needed most of all: to be clean again.

Clean-shaven and hot-water-washed in a rooming-house tub, the cowboy acted out his classic role as a free spender and hard drinker. True, cowboys on a trail's-end spree sometimes gave in to a drunken compulsion to demonstrate their manhood with six-shooters. But even though gunplay somehow came to be the gaudiest and most popular symbol of the cowboy, the classic gunfight was virtually the invention of pulp novelists and 19th-century journalists. Few such shootouts ever occurred. Most gunfights were not between cowboys but among the gamblers, toughs and professional criminals, who walk the dark corridors of any society.

Cowboys, like other 19th-

century Americans, reveled in the glamorized image of the Old West. Some came to enjoy their swashbuckling image so much that they went to elaborate ends to construct incidents of phony violence for the benefit of gullible visitors from the East.

One favorite gambit in railroad towns was the fake lynching. Cowpuncher Teddy Blue Abbott recalled an impromptu performance that he and some fellow hands put on near the Fort Kearny station of the Union Pacific Railroad. They made a dummy, placed a noose around its neck and, just as a train pulled in, threw the rope over the crossbar of a telegraph pole and jerked it into the air. As the appalled passengers gaped, the "vigilantes" fired away at the swaying dummy, shot the rope in two and proceeded to drag their straw victim across the plain at a full gallop, continuing to riddle it with bullets. Aboard the train, women fainted, children screamed and a public-spirited passenger raced into the station to telegraph news of the mayhem to the Nebraska state capital.

The code of the West had now become part of the larger legend. And some canny busi-

nessmen realized this legend was a marketable commodity. Among the first to profit were the publishers of dime novels. They treated their readers to a barrage of paperbound books about Western derring-do. A few promoters, like William F. (Buffalo Bill) Cody, entertained Eastern audiences with cowboys in the flesh. These live-action shows, along with the

romanticized reports of Western travelers, forever fixed the popular image of the cowboy's glamorous life.

The cowboys, of course, continued to cooperate in the making of their own myth. Modesty was not a part of the cowboy character, for meek men did not last long on the Great Plains. And if, in trying to live up to their image as heroes of this country's boldest legend, cowboys reached a little high for a share of immortality, it was only because they thought they deserved it. Perhaps they did.

Number of Words: 1898 ÷ _____ Minutes Reading Time = Rate _____

I. AUTHOR'S PURPOSE

Check √ the three phrases below that help explain why the author wrote the story.

_____ **1.** to describe his experiences as a cowboy

_____ **2.** to tell us how cowboys really lived

_____ **3.** to describe how cowboys saw themselves

_____ **4.** to give us an idea of the work that cowboys did

_____ **5.** to show us why Western movies are so popular

_____ **6.** to make more people want to pursue a career as a cowboy

10 points for each correct answer   SCORE: _____

II. FACT/OPINION

Some of the sentences below express facts, others opinions that may or may not be true. Write F for each sentence that states a fact, and O for each that gives an opinion.

_____ **1.** The cowboy's great years lasted for only one generation, from the mid-1860's until the mid-1880's.

_____ **2.** A cowboy without his horse was "just a plain bow-legged man who smelled horsy and slept in his underwear."

_____ **3.** The look and smell of a cowboy's bunkhouse made it immediately recognizable.

_____ **4.** The cowboy was the aristocrat among the workingmen of the West.

5 points for each correct answer   SCORE: _____

III. VOCABULARY

Circle the letter (a, b or c) of the definition that matches the meaning of the italicized word in each of the sentences below.

1. Many cowboys were *mustered-out* soldiers.
   a. undisciplined   **b.** discharged   **c.** courageous
2. Cowboys reserved their most *reverent* feelings for women.
   a. obvious   **b.** sincere   **c.** respectful
3. Cowboys accepted the *raw-edged* routine of their lives.
   a. harsh   **b.** boring   **c.** exciting
4. Cowboys came to enjoy their *swashbuckling* image.
   a. silly   **b.** daredevil   **c.** loathesome

5 points for each correct answer   SCORE: _____

IV. CHARACTERIZATION

Check √ the three statements below that describe the character of cowboys as presented in the story.

_____ **1.** Cowboys were proud of the hard life they led.

_____ **2.** A special bond existed between cowboys and their horses.

_____ **3.** Cowboys found satisfaction in meeting tough challenges.

_____ **4.** Cowboys treated everyone with contempt.

_____ **5.** Cowboys saw themselves as a special breed of men.

10 points for each correct answer   SCORE: _____

PERFECT TOTAL SCORE: 100   TOTAL SCORE: _____

V. QUESTION FOR THOUGHT

Why do you think that cowboys and their way of life were transformed into the legend we see today in books and movies?

The Spirit of a Heritage

David C. Driskell

In 1876, Edward Mitchell Bannister (1828–1901), a black painter from Providence, R. I., and Edmonia Lewis (c. 1843–1900), a black sculptor from Boston, Mass., then living in Rome, submitted works to the nation's Centennial Exposition in Philadelphia. Much to the surprise of both artists, their works were accepted and exhibited. Bannister won a medal in painting for his celebrated landscape, *Under the Oaks*. Miss Lewis submitted a marble sculpture called *The Dying Cleopatra*. It too received an award. Bannister went to the exhibit to accept his award. When he appeared,

A portrait of Edmonia Lewis

"Wooing of Hiawatha," from the statuette by Edmonia Lewis

he was told that a mistake must have been made. A mulatto, he was about to be turned away from an event in which he had been singled out to receive one of the most important honors ever to be bestowed on a living American artist. Reason prevailed, however, and Bannister was allowed into the exhibition.

Edward Bannister and Edmonia Lewis are two of many black artists who have contributed to American visual arts. Only recently has proper recognition been given to the rich visual culture black Americans brought with them from Africa and developed here.

The diversity of artistic skills brought by Africans to these shores was far-ranging. "Woodworkers" (actually sculptors), builders, ironsmiths, textile artisans, potters and goldsmiths arrived here and helped found a crafts tradition in our nation.

Blacks immediately began to make contributions to plantation architecture and folk crafts. Slaves exercised their artistic skills and used tradi-

"The Banjo Lesson" by Henry Tanner

tional African designs used on some plantation houses. From these illiterate slave-artisans came artists and craftsmen whose works, if not their stations, were the equal of any produced in America during the period.

Skilled carpenters of African ancestry were eagerly sought during the 18th and 19th centuries to make cabinets and furniture and to design and build homes, churches and public buildings. A prominent Mississippi landowner, J. M. Gibson, wrote in his memoirs that "a Negro mechanic slave" designed and supervised the construction of the Vicksburg courthouse, a landmark of historic significance built prior to the Civil War.

As early as 1825, Thomas Day, one of the most widely regarded furniture makers of the post-Colonial period, had established his reputation among craftsmen in the southeastern part of the country. He commanded handsome prices for fine furniture, mostly of imported mahogany, made in his shop in Milton, North Carolina.

African artists coming to America were not, however, trained in the fine art of traditional European painting. The art of painting portraits, landscapes and still life was not a common practice among Africans living in the sub-Sahara regions.

Despite this difference in heritage, America has produced black painters of unique gifts and distinction. One of these artists was Robert S. Duncanson (1817–1872). Duncanson's craft was so outstanding, his paintings were collected by European royalty. He made several visits to Great Britain where his work was widely acclaimed by critics who felt that he was among the finest landscape artists living in the Western world.

Another was Bannister. A true romanticist, this artist attempted in his landscapes to paint a world that reflected both the real natural world he saw and the world of his imagination. Bannister's passion was artistic questions and not social issues. While he was aware of the evils of slavery and segregation, he sought first to prove himself to be an artist whose talent could be looked upon as inferior to none.

Edmonia Lewis' concerns and style were altogether different. Her work followed the neo-classicist tradition, at the same time reflecting both her racial heritage and her classical training in Rome. But, unlike Bannister, Lewis was an artist of social comment whose subjects were timely and relevant. She created works with titles that reflected the black American heritage of her parents. *The Dying Cleopatra*, for example, was intended to show that the people of Egypt were a vital force in the history of the African continent.

The art of Henry O. Tanner (1859–1937) is more widely known than that of any other black American artist. Black Americans were not yet free when he was born in Pittsburgh on June 21, 1859. His religious upbringing and his exposure to French painting, particularly the entries he saw at the Paris Salon in 1892, determined the direction of his art.

By 1894 Tanner was well-known in the art circles of Paris and his paintings were sought by American collectors as well. His *Return from the Crucifixion, The Raising of Lazarus, The Annunciation,* and *Three Marys* were painted with masterly skill. The Art Institute of Chicago purchased his *Two Disciples at The Tomb* in 1906. That same year, *Christ at the Home of Mary and Martha* was bought by the Carnegie Institute Museum of Arts in Pittsburgh.

Meanwhile, in the United States in the 1920's, black Americans began asserting

Artist Tanner

their interest in full cultural and racial emancipation. After the end of World War I, a large number of black Americans left rural areas of the South and New York's Harlem became the center for black American culture. It was a city within a city, which gave a new voice to writers, poets, musicians and painters. Writers and poets, among them such outstanding ones as Langston Hughes and Claude McKay, were in the vanguard of those who came to develop and share their talent and expectations. Musicians from all walks of life came from as far away as San Francisco and the cities of the Deep South to share in this renaissance.

Most promising among the young artists who came to Harlem was Aaron Douglas, an artist whose freshly painted images were a welcome relief to those who had been searching for new black forms. Douglas believed that the ancestral arts of Africa were the key to a new black esthetic, a synthesis of form and style which would foster racial pride.

During the 1930s, artists such as Hale Woodruff, William E. Scott, Charles Alston and Charles White painted murals that touched upon the history and heritage of the black man in America. In their work, done mostly for public buildings and black colleges, black people, for the first time in the history of American culture, saw themselves through the eyes of their own artists. They were no longer painted as strange and tragic creatures of circumstance as they so often had been by white artists.

These years were a time of growth and movement for many black artists. The encouragement which they received from the Harmon Foundation and later the WPA allowed the work of many unknown artists to come to the attention of the public. The renaissance had been a healthy beginning. Artists of all media left Harlem— some returned to the South, others went to the Midwest. They organized art centers where large populations of black people lived. Prominent black colleges and universities such as Atlanta, Fisk and Howard founded art departments and added major curricula in the visual and performing arts to already existing programs of liberal studies. Some of these institutions invited black writers, painters, sculptors and musicians to serve on their campuses as artists-in-residence.

Many artists whose works matured during the period of social ferment now associated with the WPA and post-World War II developed into painters of great skill and creativity. Some of these artists took as their subjects the black experience. They inspired younger artists to reflect in their own work the history and heritage of their African past.

Other artists, however, did not feel the need to draw upon black American and African themes. Even artists such as Lois Jones, Palmer Hayden and Aaron Douglas, who during the Harlem renaissance had helped develop the esthetic of an art of black subjects and style, went to Europe in search of personal subjects.

Still other contemporary black artists do not even use the designs that have become recognizable as typical elements of a black style of art. Artists such as Sam Gilliam, Alma Thomas, Richard Hunt, Adrianne Hoard and William T. Williams have created work in modern styles that are also of interest to non-black artists. On the other hand, the ethnic influences that are evident in the art of William H. Johnson, William Artis, Jacob Lawrence, Romare Bearden and Charles White have left important, lasting impressions on the art of many of the young black artists. These painters use an imagery tied directly to neo-African symbols. Outstanding among those who best represent the tradition of the ethnic symbolists are Ben Jones, Keith Morrison, John Scott, Earl Hooks, Raymond Saunders, Nelson Stevens, Betty Sayre, Vincent Smith, Floyd Coleman and Claude Lockhart Clark.

These artists are basically interested in expressing their own experiences as blacks and present social conditions than in searching for new approaches to technique. The most successful black painters and sculptors working today have taken the black man as their subject matter. They paint their subject in a variety of styles, but the spirit of their work is guided by human questions more than esthetic issues. This spirit seems one that will influence black artists for some time.

Number of Words: 1516 ÷ _____ Minutes Reading Time = Rate _____

I. CLASSIFYING

Each of the following artists in column A is identified with one of the descriptions in column B. Match them by writing the correct letter in the space provided below.

	A		B
_____ **1.**	Robert S. Duncanson	**a.**	murals
_____ **2.**	Edmonia Lewis	**b.**	sculptures
_____ **3.**	Hale Woodruff	**c.**	French
_____ **4.**	Edward Mitchell Bannister	**d.**	Romanticist
_____ **5.**	Henry O. Tanner	**e.**	landscapes

6 points for each correct answer   SCORE: _____

II. STORY ELEMENTS

The author writes about some of the influences that have shaped the works of black artists. Check ✓ the four sentences that explain how he does this.

_____ **1.** He shows how the neoclassic tradition influenced one black artist.

_____ **2.** He cites the tradition of portrait painting among Africans south of the Sahara.

_____ **3.** He names the diversity of artistic skills brought by Africans to America.

_____ **4.** He indicates how a religious upbringing and training in French painting influenced another black artist.

_____ **5.** He explains how World War I determined the theme of many black artists.

_____ **6.** He cites the history of the black American as the theme of a group of black artists.

5 points for each correct answer   SCORE: _____

III. INFERENCES

Check ✓ *the three sentences below that can be* inferred *from the selection.*

_____ **1.** Black artists are mostly influenced by the oppression of the race.

_____ **2.** The works of black artists bear many influences.

_____ **3.** The work of any given artist may be traced to certain influences on his or her life.

_____ **4.** Only those black artists identifying with the black experience have become famous.

_____ **5.** The most successful black painters today deal with the subject of the human spirit.

10 points for each correct answer   SCORE: _____

IV. GENERALIZATIONS

Check ✓ *the two statements below that are* generally *true.*

_____ **1.** All black artists treat the black experience as their subject.

_____ **2.** Black artists have used various subjects and techniques in expressing themselves.

_____ **3.** One result of the Harlem Renaissance was the growth and appreciation of black art by black Americans.

10 points for each correct answer   SCORE: _____

PERFECT TOTAL SCORE: 100   TOTAL SCORE: _____

V. QUESTIONS FOR THOUGHT

What is the primary role of an artist? Of a black artist?

Bridges...Are When You Cross Them

Melvin B. Shaffer

Characters

DAD
MOTHER
SISTER
BROTHER
LITTLE FELLA

SCENE I

SCENE: *A hotel room in San Francisco. It is one of a two-room accommodation. There is an exit to the outside and also an exit to the other room of the suite. At Stage Left there is a window, near which is mounted a telescope. Next to the telescope there is a small table bearing a tourbook of the city, a notebook and several maps and diagrams. Another table in the rear section of the Stage bears an unusual burden of souvenirs, such as garish pillows, silver plates, paperweights/and all the useless things ever brought home from a vacation trip. There is a bulletin board very prominently displayed with the inscription "Family Minute Minder" boldly across the top. All the names of the members of the family are listed on the board opposite columns marked "In," "Out," "Time," etc.*

AT RISE: *We discover Dad standing at Stage Left, looking through the telescope. He is alternately referring to the maps and the tourbook and searching the city through the telescope.*

DAD: *(Reading from tourbook.)* "Located on historic and elegant Nob Hill, the Hotel Mark Hopkins is famous for its world-renowned dining room in the clouds, the "Top of the Mark." *(He checks the map again and then looks through the telescope again.)* Yep. By George, that's it, all right. *(As he writes in notebook and consults watch.)* Hotel Mark Hopkins: 6:45 p.m. Well, that's another one out of the way. *(Again reading from tourbook.)* "San Francisco is a bridge between the cultures of the East and West. It is a bridge between the traditions of the gracious living of yesterday and the dynamic new world of the future."

(MOTHER and LITTLE FELLA enter.)

MOTHER: You're early. You weren't due this early, were you? *(She goes immediately to the "Minute Minder" to check his schedule and to sign in. She then helps LITTLE FELLA to do the same.)* You weren't due back until 7:00.

DAD: That's right, 7:00. But I was falling behind schedule, so I came back to the hotel to catch some of the higher spots from the window. Just about finished now.

MOTHER: Good idea, the telescope. Lucky thing we brought it along.

DAD: Yes, indeed, it certainly is. Have a good day, dear?

MOTHER: Oh, yes. I should say. Very nice. Do you know that I believe this city is a kind of bridge between the gracious living of yesterday and the dynamic new world of the future?

DAD: Yes, I suppose it is, dear.

LITTLE FELLA: Hi, Dad.

DAD: Hi, Little Fella.

MOTHER: (To LITTLE FELLA.) Come on. You have to nap before dinner. (To DAD.) Eight minutes, honey.

(DAD sets the alarm clock for eight minutes. MOTHER and LITTLE FELLA exit to the bedroom. DAD goes back to his telescope and scans around in something of a quandary.)

DAD: By George! That's funny.

MOTHER: (As she reenters.) What's funny?

DAD: The bridge. I thought we'd be able to see the Golden Gate Bridge from here.

MOTHER: Maybe we're not high enough.

DAD: The clerk said we were. It ought to be right over that way.

MOTHER: Let me have a look. (MOTHER looks through the telescope.) No. Nothing there that I can see.

DAD: Funny, isn't it? (He checks the map again.) Well, it's not that important, I guess. Can't waste the whole evening over it.

MOTHER: I suppose you're right, dear. No use doing double work, is there? Who's got the bridge?

DAD: Brother.

MOTHER: Good. He'll do a good job with it.

DAD: No worries there, by George. The boy has what it takes. Give him an assignment, and it'll be done. No doubt about that.

MOTHER: He has a fine sense of discipline.

DAD: Right. Been a perfect trouper on this whole vacation. Accurate, thorough reports.

MOTHER: He's a good boy. . . . By the way, he's bringing the dinner tonight—Chinese food.

DAD: Fine. Fine. We'll eat well, then. If Brother is bringing the dinner, we'll eat well, no worries there. He's really making the most of this trip, isn't he?

MOTHER: He certainly is. He's been a perfect gem. All through Seattle, Portland, Los Angeles, Disneyland, San Simeon, Yosemite, Monterey, Carmel . . .

DAD: Yes, it's been a very successful week, hasn't it?

MOTHER: It really has. The children have been
          so efficient. Except for Sister, they've been practi-
          cally perfect.

DAD: I'm afraid if Sister isn't careful, she'll get a
          failing grade for the whole trip. She doesn't seem
          to understand the importance of teamwork. The
          trip is just not meaningful without teamwork.
          (Looks at the Minute Minder.) Where is she?
          (Looks at watch.) She's late. Late again. Due in at
          6:45. Where in the world is that girl? Five minutes
          in Seattle, eight at Yellowstone. It's getting worse
          all the time.

MOTHER: I've been so worried about her, honey.

DAD: Just not reliable.

MOTHER: I worry now every time she goes out alone.

DAD: We deliberately gave her a light assignment, and
          still she's late. Not reliable. Show me a man
          who is late for appointments, and, by George, I'll
          show you a man who is never a reliable team
          player.

MOTHER: Maybe it isn't all her fault. I think she tries, I
          really do. But she just seems . . .

(The following is recited as though reading a school report card.)

MOTHER: Unable to discipline herself—

DAD: Does not put forth best effort—

MOTHER: Cannot keep her mind on her work—

DAD: Seems unwilling to cooperate—

MOTHER: Has a tendency to daydream—

DAD: Does not work well with others—

MOTHER: Times late: Three—

DAD: Times absent: None. . . . At least in body. The
          mind is something else again. Absent most of the
          time, it seems. Daydreaming! Fantasies!

MOTHER: I sometimes wonder if we're doing the right
          thing. Maybe we're not paying enough attention to
          Sister. I've been so worried about what happened
          in Seattle.

DAD: Seattle! SEATTLE!! I don't want to talk about Seattle any more. You don't humor a child about something like that. Best thing is for everyone to forget all about it. . . . Now I've got to firm up the schedules for Denver and Central City tomorrow.

(DAD *exits into the bedroom.* MOTHER *now crosses to the window and searches the horizon through the telescope. She obviously comes up blank.*)

MOTHER: That is strange! (SISTER *enters. She has been running, and her hair is quite wind-blown and her face flushed.*) Where in the world have you been? Just look at you. You're all out of breath. Your hair is a mess.

SISTER: I've been running. I was afraid I would be late, so I ran.

MOTHER: You are late.

SISTER: Am I?

MOTHER: Don't try to play games with me, young lady. You're late and you know it.

SISTER: Is Dad very angry?

MOTHER: He's not very pleased, I can tell you. . . . *(Softening to her.)* But not so very angry, either. *(Very kindly now.)* Sister, I've been wondering. How would you like it if we went out together for the rest of the trip? If we combined our sight-seeing assignments, you and I?

SISTER: Oh, Mother, could we? I'd love it. Wouldn't it be much more fun to see things together?

MOTHER: I'll speak to Dad about Denver and Central City. I think it might be better if we stay together. I've felt this ever since Seattle.

SISTER: Seattle! Oh, that's the reason you want to go with me. You don't really want to see things together at all. You just want to keep an eye on me. You just want to watch me like a child, don't you?

MOTHER: I do not want to watch you like a child. It's just that if we were together, I don't think things like . . . like that would happen any more.

SISTER: Nothing "happened," Mother. I simply saw it. I really did, regardless of what everyone else says. I know you don't believe me, but I did. I wouldn't have brought you all back to look at it if I hadn't seen it myself, would I? It was there, and I saw it. That's all there was to it.

MOTHER: We've been all through this before. Let's not have it again. Let's put it out of our minds once and for all. And above all, don't dare mention it to your father again. I'm afraid he still believes you were telling an untruth, and you know how he feels about that. . . . I don't agree with him, mind you, but I think it would be better if you stayed with me. Everything will be all right once we get home, I'm sure of that.

SISTER: What do you mean everything *will be* all right? Everything is all right *now*, Mother.

(The ALARM rings.)

MOTHER: I've got to wake Little Fella. Come along now and get yourself ready for dinner. Your hair looks like it hasn't seen a comb in a month.

SISTER: All right, Mother.

(MOTHER *exits to the bedroom.* SISTER *crosses to the window and begins to look through the telescope. She seems to find what she is looking for and stares at it, smiling.* BROTHER *enters from the outside. Goes immediately to the Minute Minder to sign in.*)

SISTER: Hey, what have you got in the bag? M-m-m-m! Smells good. Let's see.

BROTHER: No. That's our dinner. You're supposed to wait until dinner time.

SISTER: Stingy! What is it?

BROTHER: It's a surprise. It's real Chinese food, though, I can tell you that much. But you'll have to wait like everybody else.

(MOTHER *and* DAD *enter from the bedroom, talking.*)

DAD: It's pointless. And besides, the schedule is all worked out. *(To* BROTHER.*)* Ah, have a good day, Brother?

MOTHER: Of course he did.

BROTHER: Yes, Dad. Of course I did.

DAD: Of course you did. How do you like San Francisco?

BROTHER: I think it's a very nice place to visit, but I wouldn't want to live here.

DAD: Very well put.

BROTHER: Here's the food, Mother. *(Hands* MOTHER *the packages.)*

MOTHER: Oh, fine. My, it smells good. . . . You'd better wash up now.

*(*BROTHER *exits to the bedroom.)*

DAD: *(To* SISTER.*)* Just look at you! You're a mess. Where in the world have you been?

SISTER: *(Trying to smooth her hair.)* It was the wind, I guess. I was . . .

DAD: *(Interrupting her.)* You're late again. *(Looks at the Minute Minder.)* In fact, you're not even here yet according to the Minute Minder.

*(*SISTER *goes to the board to sign in under* DAD's *reproving stare.)*

SISTER: It was only a few minutes, Dad.

DAD: Minutes add up to hours, and hours to weeks and weeks to years. A wasted minute is a wasted life.

SISTER: Yes, Dad, I know. I'm sorry. I didn't realize the time. It just skipped by, I guess.

DAD: Must never let time skip by us.

MOTHER: Time is money. . . . Now come on. Comb your hair. Hurry.

*(*SISTER *exits hurriedly through the bedroom door.)*

DAD: Complete disorganization. The girl is completely disorganized.

MOTHER: That's why I thought it would be better to keep

her with me tomorrow. Help her get back into the routine.

DAD: No, dear. It's out of the question. We've worked out the schedule, and we can't change it now. Everybody on the team has got to keep his nose to the grindstone until we bring down the curtain on this whole kettle of fish.

MOTHER: What did you say, dear?

DAD: Never mind. She's got a schedule of sights to see, and she's going to see them, by George. Besides, it's self discipline she needs. Can't go on doing her thinking for her forever. She's got to learn sooner or later. Got to learn to think for herself. Got to learn to respect the truth.

MOTHER: Yes, I know. But she did seem so confused in Seattle.

DAD: She was not confused in Seattle. She was lying.

MOTHER: I don't think she was lying. I think she actually thought she saw it. Imagined it.

DAD: Impossible. We were all standing right there with her, and none of us saw it. By George, if that's her idea of a joke. . . . Dragging us all the way down there—wasting a whole hour—for nothing. Embarrassing. . . . Her standing there looking at the sky and screaming that we must all be blind. By George, if that's her idea of a joke—

MOTHER: No, I don't think she meant it as a joke. And she wasn't lying. I think she really believed it.

DAD: Nonsense. There's nothing wrong with Sister. She's not sick. She's prefectly healthy. How could she believe such a thing?

MOTHER: But what about all the publicity? What about the pictures in the tourbook?

DAD: Yes, I saw the pictures. Very clever. Good grief, Mother! You don't believe it, too?

MOTHER: No. No, of course not. But couldn't that explain it? Maybe she read the tourbooks so often that she began to believe it. Couldn't that be it?

DAD: Well, I don't—

MOTHER: Maybe she was just caught up in the publicity of it. A kind of . . . of mass hysteria.

DAD: Mass hysteria. M-m-m-m. No, I doubt it. Anyway, that would be all the more reason for her to discipline her mind . . . to question impossible things. If she'd used her common sense, she would have known that a thing like that couldn't possibly exist. A ridiculous-looking thing like that. Why, it couldn't even stand up. It would topple over.

MOTHER: But if she were to come with me tomorrow—

DAD: It's out of the question. We've got to follow the schedule as it is.

LITTLE FELLA: (*Has wandered in from the bedroom during this conversation and has been overhearing a great deal of it.*) What's the matter with Sister?

MOTHER: Nothing. Nothing is the matter with her. Why do you think that?

LITTLE FELLA: She sure acts funny.

MOTHER: She just has an overactive imagination, that's all.

LITTLE FELLA: What's *overactive*?

MOTHER: *Overactive* is when you have too much of something.

LITTLE FELLA: What's *imagination*?

MOTHER: Well, it's . . . like in fairy tales.

LITTLE FELLA: What's *fairy tales*?

MOTHER: Oh, yes . . . well, Little Fella, it's make-believe.

LITTLE FELLA: Make-believe?

MOTHER: *Make-believe* is . . . is having an overactive imagination.

LITTLE FELLA: Oh.

(DAD *consults his watch and summons them to dinner. They* ALL *appear immediately except* SISTER, *who is a shade later than the others. She enters to their reproving glances.*)

SISTER: (*Explaining her tardiness.*) Brother got to the bathroom first.

DAD: (*Considers the excuse. It is a good one.*) Fine. That's a perfectly acceptable excuse.

(DAD *taps his water glass with a fork. They* ALL *sit on signal. He taps again and they fold their hands for the blessing.*

BROTHER: Arebus sane, aforbus sane, aversify, f'sake, Amen.

MOTHER: Now, what have we for dinner? . . . Oh, Chop Suey!

DAD: Great! By George, Chinese food. Now, Brother, first, tell us about the restaurant.

BROTHER: There are many restaurants in Chinatown. I went to one called the "New Dragon Lady." It has Chinese writing in the window . . . in red neon. And then inside there is a gold Buddha, just like you would find in China, right before you get to the soda fountain. And that was certainly interesting. The waiters are all Chinese and they wear red coats. The people who eat in the restaurant are not Chinese, except for a Chinese girl who sits at the soda fountain and winks at people coming in.

MOTHER: That *is* interesting.

SISTER: Did you wink back? (*She winks at him playfully.*)

DAD: Fine report, Brother, fine report. That's the way to set up a meal. It's practically the same as being right in China.

SISTER: I wish we could have eaten in Chinatown.

DAD: Sister!

SISTER: Oh, I know we don't have the time. But it would have been fun, wouldn't it? Wouldn't you like to try some of the other dishes? I would. I mean the kind we can't get back home. I'd really like that. That would be even better than eating in the Space Needle Restaurant.

(SISTER *realizes her slip as they all stop eating and stare at her in shocked silence.*)

DAD: The *what?*

BROTHER: She still believes it. She still believes it. Mother, Dad, I told you she still believes it. Saw a Space Needle, ha, ha, ha!

LITTLE FELLA: Sister saw a Space Needle, ha, ha, ha!

SISTER: You shut up!

MOTHER: Quiet, boys. Sister, I think that will be about enough nonsense. Eat your dinner, and let's not talk any more about it.

SISTER: But I did see it, Mother. Honest, I did. And I just saw another picture of it in the newspaper yesterday. Everyone else says it's there.

MOTHER: I thought we were through with this. I thought we had decided that there is simply no such thing as a Space Needle.

SISTER: But, Mother! I—

DAD: That will be enough! There will be no more mention of the Space Needle or any other imaginary monstrosities in this family. . . . Mother!

(MOTHER *goes to the bedroom door and opens it. The* CHILDREN *get up and file somberly into the bedroom in a familiar ritual.* MOTHER *closes the door.)*

DAD: Darn! (MOTHER *opens the door and the* CHILDREN *file back and take their places.)* Now. I think we'll enjoy our vacation more if we concentrate on what we saw today and let the past remain in the past. We must work together. That's the important thing about vacations—teamwork. Now, Sister, let's have your report.

SISTER: I'd rather wait, Dad. I mean, I think—*(She is stalling.)*

DAD: Nonsense, it's your turn. What did we see today through your eyes?

SISTER: Well, I saw . . . I saw the city.

MOTHER: What did you like best, Sister?

SISTER: What I liked best of all was . . . *(She hesitates. She didn't mean to tell this.)* . . . the ocean.

MOTHER: The ocean?

DAD: It isn't even on the schedule. We decided we wouldn't have time for it.

SISTER: But I've never seen the ocean.

MOTHER: What is there to see? Nothing but water. You see the Platt River day in and day out at home, and that's water. Quite enough water, I should think.

SISTER: But this is the ocean, Mother. The Pacific Ocean. Don't you see? It is the same ocean that goes all the way to Hawaii and Tahiti and even farther. Thousands and thousands of miles of it, and it touches the city. Comes right up to the city. I wish you could have seen it. I went all the way down to the beach and took off my shoes and even put my feet into the ocean. And then I ran along the beach in the sand until I felt like I would just take off and fly.

MOTHER: *(Apprehensively.)* That's very interesting.

DAD: But, Sister, you had the museums.

SISTER: *(Not hearing him.)* And then I walked along the—

DAD: *(Interrupting.)* The museums! Let's stick to the official sights.

SISTER: The museums? The museums. *(Begins to bluff it.)* Well, the first was the uh—*(Stops and confesses.)* I didn't go to the museums, Dad.

DAD: You didn't *what?* Do you mean to say that we missed the museums? Do you mean to say that you wasted the whole day—a precious day—just daydreaming at the ocean? Do you mean to tell us that we missed centuries of culture just because of your selfishness? (DAD *has become extremely excited and agitated and* MOTHER *tries to placate him.)* Mother!

(MOTHER *goes to the bedroom door and opens it again. The* CHILDREN *solemnly file through it.* DAD *looks at* MOTHER *and motions her in also.)*

MOTHER: That bad?

(DAD *nods yes.* MOTHER *goes into the bedroom and closes the door after her.)*

DAD: Darn! Darn!

(DAD *has been purged. He is once again in good spirits. He goes back to his chair and sits. The door opens and they all file back*

*into the room and take their places quietly. They sit for a moment
in silence.)*

DAD: Now, Brother. We've all been waiting. The Golden Gate Bridge.

BROTHER: *(Stands to recite, using notes.)* The Golden Gate Bridge actually crosses over a portion of the Pacific Ocean. It is the longest single-span suspension bridge in the entire world, and that certainly is interesting. I took the bus directly to the bridge. There were lots of people going to the bridge.

MOTHER: Is it really red as they say?

SISTER: It is beautiful, isn't it?

DAD: What time did you see it?

BROTHER: I arrived there at 2:18 p.m. But the most interesting thing of all about the bridge is that it isn't there.

SISTER: What do you mean, it isn't there?

BROTHER: It just isn't there. The bridge isn't there. I looked and looked everywhere, but I didn't see it.

SISTER: You didn't see it?

DAD: Now, Brother. Are you quite sure you didn't see it?

BROTHER: Yes, Dad, I'm sure. And I looked very carefully, too.

MOTHER: What about all the other people on the bus? Could they see it?

BROTHER: They were all looking in the same direction at something. I suppose they had all read the tour-book, too.

DAD: *(Going to the telescope.)* That explains it, then. Yes, by George, that explains it. I began to suspect it when neither Mother nor I could see it.

BROTHER: I couldn't see it through the telescope, either. I tried.

DAD: We'd better make sure, though. It's a serious matter. Look again.

BROTHER: *(Looks through the telescope.)* I don't see a thing, Dad.

DAD: Mother.

MOTHER: *(Looks through the telescope.)* No, nothing.

DAD: Little fella.

LITTLE FELLA: *(As he looks.)* Nope.

DAD: Sister. (SISTER *looks through the telescope. She is obviously very shaken by what she sees, but turns away without saying anything.)* Well, Sister? (SISTER *does not answer. She merely nods her head indeterminately.)* Well, that should settle it. There is no such thing as the Golden Gate Bridge.

MOTHER: Oh, dear. What a disappointment!

DAD: I think this is a good lesson for us to remember. You've got to be careful in this world not to believe all you hear or read. Got to discover for yourself what is real and what is not. Can't go along with the mob. Got to be an individual. Got to think for yourself.

SISTER: I saw it, Dad.

DAD: Saw what?

SISTER: The bridge. The Golden Gate Bridge. . . . I did see it. I swear I did.

DAD: Do you mean to stand there and tell me—?

SISTER: Please don't be angry with me. I did see it.

DAD: It's Seattle all over again.

SISTER: I can still see it. Look! Look! Please look. Please say you can see it, too.

DAD: Now get hold of yourself and use a little common sense. You know perfectly well that it isn't there.

MOTHER: You are imagining it, Sister.

SISTER: No. I'm not imagining it. It is there. I see it. Mother, you believe me, don't you?

MOTHER: I believe you think you see it, dear.

SISTER: No, I *do* see it. It's real. Why won't you listen to me? Today—today . . . I tried to tell you before but you wouldn't listen. . . . Today I was actually standing on the bridge. I was, Dad, please believe me. Why don't you come with me and I'll show you?

DAD: Into the other room, boys. (BROTHER *and* LITTLE FELLA *exit into the bedroom.)* Now, Sister. This has gone about far enough. Seattle was bad, but

this is worse. I will not have you disrupting the family with your wild tales. If this is your idea of a joke, it is not a very funny one.

MOTHER: And if you really believe this, then you are not well.

SISTER: *(Horrified.)* Oh, no! You don't think that. That's not true. Mother, it's not true. I'm all right. I'll prove it to you. I'll prove the bridge is there. *(She runs out the door toward the street.)*

MOTHER: *(Sternly.)* Sister! You come back here this minute. (SISTER *has not even heard her. To* DAD.) Don't let her go. Stop her!

DAD: Let her go. She'll be back in two minutes. Nasty temper, that's all. . . .

MOTHER: *(Has gone to the window as if by premonition— she is quite alarmed. Suddenly she begins staring in horror.)* There! It is there! She was right, it is there! Stop her! Stop her!

(END OF SCENE I)

SCENE II

AT RISE: *As the* LIGHTS *come up, there is no one on the Stage.* BROTHER *and* LITTLE FELLA *are still in the bedroom.* MOTHER *and* DAD *enter from the outside.* MOTHER *is still worried and anxious, but* DAD *appears to be quite calm if stern.*

MOTHER: Maybe she came back. *(Goes to the bedroom door and calls out.)* Did Sister come back yet?

BROTHER: *(Off.)* No, Mother.

DAD: Now, dear, just calm down. The police will find her all right. (MOTHER *goes to the window and looks through the telescope apprehensively.)* And as far as that is concerned, you know perfectly well there is nothing to worry about. She can't very well jump off a bridge that doesn't exist, now, can she?

MOTHER: No, you're right. It isn't there now. But I could

have sworn I saw it before.

DAD: *(Opens the bedroom door.)* Okay, boys. Front and center. (BROTHER *and* LITTLE FELLA *enter from the bedroom.)* Now, Mother. The department stores. That's your department. Heh, heh, heh. Excuse the joke.

(The BOYS *laugh obediently.)*

MOTHER: We went through all the department stores. There are seven major ones. But they really don't have anything that you can't find at the . . . *(To* DAD.) Don't you think we should have heard something by now?

DAD: Not necessarily.

MOTHER: . . . At the Ranchleigh Shopping Center, except that the prices are much higher. . . . Maybe we'd better call them.

DAD: No point in it. They promised to call us.

MOTHER: Then we rode the cable car. The cable cars are very interesting. They were invented—*(She is interrupted by* SISTER'S *entrance.* SISTER *seems very calm and in marked contrast to her frantic exit at the end of the last scene.* MOTHER *goes to her and embraces her.)* Oh, thank heavens! Are you all right, Sister? Are you all right?

SISTER: Yes, Mother. I'm all right. I'm fine. *(Crosses immediately to the window.)*

DAD: Did the police find you?

SISTER: The police? No.

DAD: I hope you're not going to ask us to look at that bridge again.

SISTER: No, Dad. I'm not going to ask you that.

MOTHER: Can you . . . can you still see it?

SISTER: No, not now. All I can see is the fog now.

MOTHER: Where in the world have you been? We've been worried to death.

SISTER: I'm sorry I worried you, Mother. I started to go to the bridge . . . but I couldn't find it.

DAD: Good. Of course you couldn't. Well, I'm glad you

	finally realized it.
SISTER:	I took the wrong bus, I guess. I thought it was the same one I took today, but I guess it wasn't. We were riding toward the bridge all right. I could see it in the distance, but all of a sudden we turned and went off in another direction, and it just simply disappeared. I got off at the next stop and ran back.
MOTHER:	Back where?
SISTER:	Back to the top of the hill where I could see the bridge again. I kept running, but I couldn't seem to get any closer to it. I thought I was running toward it, but it would move first to the right and then to the left. Every time it moved, I tried to follow it.
MOTHER:	And every time you tried to follow it, it moved.
DAD:	Mother! You're just adding to the—
MOTHER:	Hush!
SISTER:	Once when I was running, it was right ahead of me, and I thought I was almost there, but the street ended, and I had to go all the way back. And then I lost it. It got foggy and then it got dark, and I didn't know where it was. I didn't even know where I was. . . . I'm really sorry I worried you, but I just had to see it again, Mother. . . . to know.
MOTHER:	Poor baby. How did you get back to the hotel?
SISTER:	A cab brought me. . . . I kept running. I had to, even though I didn't know which direction to go. I was crying pretty hard, I guess, and a cab pulled up and stopped. The driver wanted to know if I was all right. I jumped into the cab and told him to take me to the Golden Gate Bridge as fast as he could. I must have been practically hysterical because he said, "Now wait a minute, young lady. I don't think you really want to go there, do you?" And I told him, "Yes, yes, I do. I want to go there right away. I have to. And don't you try to tell me it isn't there." And then he said, "No. No. I'm not

going to try to tell you that. But let's not be in
such a hurry. You've got all the time in the
world."

DAD: Certainly. That's typical. Run up the meter.
That's a cab driver for you.

SISTER: Then he told me not to worry if I was in
trouble. He said that everybody makes a mistake
once in a while and that there are worse things
in life than that. And then he said he didn't
think there was much sense in going *to* a bridge.
Going *across* a bridge makes sense, but not going *to* it. And I told him that I just wanted to
see it . . . just once more.

MOTHER: Wouldn't he take you to it?

SISTER: No, he wouldn't. Do you know what he said
then? He said, "No point in going there to *see* it.
If you ever want to cross it, it'll be there. And if
you're never going to cross it, it doesn't make
any difference whether it's there or not, does
it?"

MOTHER: I wonder what in the world he meant by that.

SISTER: I think I know. I think I know now what he
meant. . . . And then we drove around for a long
time, and we talked and talked. He was very
nice. We talked about the bridge, and we talked
about the ocean, and about Tahiti and Hawaii,
and school, and Little Fella and just about
everything. We could have talked all night, but
then he brought me back to the hotel because I
was afraid you would be worried about me.

MOTHER: We certainly were.

DAD: Sister, you ought to be punished, you know that,
don't you?

SISTER: Yes, Dad, I know.

DAD: But I think you've learned a very valuable lesson
from this. Maybe we all have—a very meaning-
ful lesson. . . . There is one piece of advice I
would like to give you, though. It is the best
thing I know to help build character. Do you

know what I do when I begin to get angry? I count to ten, and then it goes away. Now, I think maybe this little rule would work for you, too. Whenever you start to imagine strange things like this, try counting to ten, and I think they'll go away.

SISTER: Don't worry, Dad. I don't think I'll have to count to ten. I don't think I'll imagine things any more.

DAD: Good. Well, you've already missed some of Mother's very interesting report.

MOTHER: No, I think maybe Sister is too tired.

SISTER: It's all right, Mother. I'm not tired at all.

DAD: The cab! You left the cab waiting. I'd better go pay him.

SISTER: No. He's already gone. He said there wouldn't be any charge. I told him to wait until I got the money, but he said he didn't want any money. He just looked at me and smiled and said he was well paid already—that it wasn't every day he saw someone cross a bridge without even touching it.

They all turn to look at SISTER, *who is smiling as she looks toward the window.)*

CURTAIN

Number of Words: 5356 ÷ _____ Minutes Reading Time = Rate _____

I. OUTLINING

Complete the outline of the play by writing the letter (a, b, c, d, e or f) for each of the following sentences in its proper place.

    a. She was often late.
    b. She saw the Golden Gate Bridge and the Space Needle.
    c. Everyone was given a schedule of places to visit.
    d. They were unable to see objects of beauty.
    e. She learned to believe in her way of seeing the world.
    f. She spent the day at the ocean instead of visiting the museum.

  I. The family tried to order every part of their vacation.
    A. They kept a Minute Minder.
    B. _____
    C. Everyone had to recite his day's activities.
 II. The family lacked imagination.
    A. They followed strict rules in their lives.
    B. _____
        1. They could not see the Space Needle when they visited Seattle.
        2. They could not see the Golden Gate Bridge when they were in San Francisco.
III. Sister did not fit in well with the family.
    A. She was more imaginative.
        1. She liked to daydream.
        2. _____
    B. She was more adventurous and independent.
        1. _____
        2. She wanted to try new things.
    C. She did not like to follow their rules.
        1. _____
        2. She forgot to sign in.
 IV. Sister crosses a bridge.
    A. _____
    B. She grew up.

10 points for each correct answer   SCORE: _____

II. MAIN IDEA

Check √ the one statement that best describes what the play is about.

_____ **1.**   A family on vacation in San Francisco discovers that the Golden Gate Bridge does not really exist.

_____ **2.**   A girl breaks away from the influence of her narrow-minded, self-righteous family.

_____ **3.**   A family organizes their activities during a vacation so that they see as many sights as possible.

20 points for the correct answer   SCORE: _____

III. REFERENCE

When planning a trip, what could you read or where could you go to obtain information about interesting places to visit? Check √ the four sources below that would be useful.

_____ **1.**   a tour book
_____ **2.**   an almanac
_____ **3.**   a travel agent
_____ **4.**   an encyclopedia
_____ **5.**   a Tourist Information Bureau
_____ **6.**   brochures from the local Historical Society

5 points for each correct answer   SCORE: _____

PERFECT TOTAL SCORE: 100   TOTAL SCORE: _____

IV. QUESTION FOR THOUGHT

In the play, Sister says she understands what the cab driver meant by, "If you ever want to cross a bridge, it'll be there. And if you're never going to cross it, it doesn't make any difference whether it's there or not." What do you understand this to mean?